ELIZABETH LINDSAY DAVIS

THE STORY OF THE ILLINOIS FEDERATION OF COLORED WOMEN'S CLUBS

MRS. S. JOE BROWN

THE HISTORY OF THE ORDER OF THE EASTERN STAR AMONG COLORED PEOPLE

AFRICAN-AMERICAN WOMEN WRITERS, 1910–1940

HENRY LOUIS GATES, JR. *GENERAL EDITOR*

Jennifer Burton *Associate Editor*

OTHER TITLES IN THIS SERIES

ELIZABETH LINDSAY DAVIS

THE STORY OF THE ILLINOIS FEDERATION OF COLORED WOMEN'S CLUBS

MRS. S. JOE BROWN

THE HISTORY OF THE ORDER OF THE EASTERN STAR AMONG COLORED PEOPLE

Introduction by
SHEILA SMITH MCKOY

G.K. HALL & CO.
An Imprint of Simon & Schuster Macmillan
New York

Prentice Hall International
London   Mexico City   New Delhi   Singapore   Sydney   Toronto

G. K. Hall & Co.
An Imprint of Simon & Schuster Macmillan
1633 Broadway
New York, NY 10019

Library of Congress Catalog Card Number: 96-44607

Printed in the United States of America

Printing Number
1 2 3 4 5 6 7 8 9 10

Library of Congress Cataloging-in-Publication Data

Davis, Elizabeth Lindsay.
    The story of the Illinois Federation of Colored Women's Clubs / Elizabeth Lindsay Davis. The history of the Order of the Eastern Star among colored people / Mrs. Joe S. Brown ; introduction by Sheila Smith McKoy.
        p.   cm.—(Africa-American women writers, 1910–1940)
    Includes bibliographical references.
    ISBN 0-7838-1422-4 (alk. paper)
    1. Illinois Federation of Colored Women's Clubs—History.   2. Afro-American women—Illinois—Societies and clubs—History.   3. Afro-American women—Illinois—Biography.   4. Order of the Easter Star-freemasonary—United States—History.   I. Brown, S. Joe, Mrs. History of the Order of the Eastern Star among colored people.
    II. Title.   III. Title : History of the Order of the Eastern Star among colored people.   IV. Series.
    E185.93.12D.38   1997
    366'.18'089960730773—dc21   96-44607
                                                                                    CIP

This paper meets the requirements of ANSI/NISO Z39.48.1992 (Permanence of Paper).

CONTENTS

GENERAL EDITORS' PREFACE

The past decade of our literary history might be thought of as the era of African-American women writers. Culminating in the awarding of the Pulitzer Prize to Toni Morrison and Rita Dove and the Nobel Prize for Literature to Toni Morrison in 1993 and characterized by the presence of several writers—Toni Morrison, Alice Walker, Maya Angelou, and the Delaney Sisters, among others—on the *New York Times* Best Seller List, the shape of the most recent period in our literary history has been determined in large part by the writings of black women.

This, of course, has not always been the case. African-American women authors have been publishing their thoughts and feelings at least since 1773, when Phillis Wheatley published her book of poems in London, thereby bringing poetry directly to bear upon the philosophical discourse over the African's "place in nature" and his or her place in the great chain of being. The scores of words published by black women in America in the nineteenth century—most of which were published in extremely limited editions and never reprinted—have been republished in new critical editions in the forty-volume *Schomburg Library of Nineteenth-Century Black Women Writers*. The critical response to that series has led to requests from scholars and students alike for a similar series, one geared to the work by black women published between 1910 and the beginning of World War Two.

African-American Women Writers, 1910–1940 is designed to bring back into print many writers who otherwise would be unknown to contemporary readers, and to increase the availability of lesser-known texts by established writers who originally published during this critical period in African-American letters. This series implicitly acts as a chronological sequel to the Schomburg series, which focused on the origins of the black female literary tradition in America.

In less than a decade, the study of African-American women's writings has grown from its promising beginnings into a firmly established field in departments of English, American Studies, and African-American Studies. A comparison of the form and function of the original series and this sequel illustrates this dramatic shift. The *Schomburg Library* was published at the cusp of focused academic investigation into the interplay between race and gender. It covered the extensive period from the publication of Phillis Wheatley's *Poems on Various Subjects, Religious and Moral* in 1773 through the "Black Women's Era" of 1890–1910, and was designed to be an inclusive series of the major early texts by black women writers. The Schomburg Library provided a historical backdrop for black women's writings of the 1970s and 1980s, including the works of writers such as Toni Morrison, Alice Walker, Maya Angelou, and Rita Dove.

African-American Women Writers, 1910–1940 continues our effort to provide a new generation of readers access to texts—historical, sociological, and literary—that have been largely "unread" for most of this century. The series bypasses works that are important both to the period and the tradition, but that are readily available, such as Zora Neale Hurston's *Their Eyes Were Watching God*, Jessie Fauset's *Plum Bun* and *There Is Confusion*, and Nella Larsen's *Quicksand* and *Passing*. Our goal is to provide access to a wide variety of rare texts. The series includes Fauset's two other novels, *The Chinaberry Tree: A Novel of American Life* and *Comedy: American Style*, and Hurston's short play *Color Struck*, since these are not yet widely available. It also features works by virtually unknown writers, such as *A Tiny Spark*, Christina Moody's slim volume of poetry self-published in 1910, and *Reminiscences of School Life, and Hints on Teaching*, written by Fanny Jackson Coppin in the last year of her life (1913), a multigenre work combining an autobiographical sketch and reflections on trips to England and South Africa, complete with pedagogical advice.

Cultural studies' investment in diverse resources allows the historic scope of the *African-American Women Writers* series to be more focused than the *Schomburg Library* series, which covered works written over a 137-year period. With few exceptions, the authors included in the *African-American Women Writers* series wrote their major works between 1910 and 1940. The texts reprinted include all the works by each particular author that are not otherwise readily obtainable. As a result, two volumes contain works originally published after 1940. The Charlotte Hawkins Brown volume includes her book of etiquette published in 1941, *The Correct Thing To Do—To Say—To Wear*. One of the poetry volumes contains Maggie Pogue Johnson's *Fallen Blossoms*, published in 1951, a compilation of all her previously published and unpublished poems.

Excavational work by scholars during the past decade has been crucial to the development of *African-American Women Writers, 1910-1940*. Germinal bibliographical sources such as Ann Allen Shockley's *Afro-American Women Writers 1746-1933* and Maryemma Graham's *Database of African-American Women Writers* made the initial identification of texts possible. Other works were brought to our attention by scholars who wrote letters sharing their research. Additional texts by selected authors were then added, so that many volumes contain the complete oeuvres of particular writers. Pieces by authors without enough published work to fill an entire volume were grouped with other pieces by genre.

The two types of collections, those organized by author and those organized by genre, bring out different characteristics of black women's writings of the period. The collected works of the literary writers illustrate that many of them were experimenting with a variety of forms. Mercedes Gilbert's volume, for example, contains her 1931 collection *Selected Gems of Poetry, Comedy, and Drama, Etc.*, as well as her 1938 novel *Aunt Sarah's Wooden God*. Georgia Douglas Johnson's volume contains her plays and short stories in addition to her poetry. Sarah Lee Brown Fleming's volume combines her 1918 novel *Hope's Highway* with her 1920 collection of poetry, *Clouds and Sunshine*.

The generic volumes both bring out the formal and thematic similarities among many of the writings and highlight the striking individuality of particular writers. Most of the plays in the volume of one-acts are social dramas whose tragic endings can be clearly attributed to miscegenation and racism. Within the context of these other plays, Marita Bonner's expressionistic theatrical vision becomes all the more striking.

The volumes of *African-American Women Writers, 1910–1940* contain reproductions of more than one hundred previously published texts, including twenty-nine plays, seventeen poetry collections, twelve novels, six autobiographies, five collections of short biographical sketches, three biographies, three histories of organizations, three black histories, two anthologies, two sociological studies, a diary, and a book of etiquette. Each volume features an introduction by a contemporary scholar that provides crucial biographical data on each author and the historical and critical context of her work. In some cases, little information on the authors was available outside of the fragments of biographical data contained in the original introduction or in the text itself. In these instances, editors have documented the libraries and research centers where they tried to find information, in the hope that subsequent scholars will continue the necessary search to find the "lost" clues to the women's stories in the rich stores of papers, letters, photographs, and other primary materials scattered throughout the country that have yet to be fully catalogued.

Many of the thrilling moments that occurred during the development of this series were the result of previously fragmented pieces of these women's histories suddenly coming together, such as Adele Alexander's uncovering of an old family photograph picturing her own aunt with Addie Hunton, the author Alexander was researching. Claudia Tate's examination of Georgia Douglas Johnson's papers in the Moorland-Spingarn Research Center of Howard University resulted in the discovery of a wealth of previously unpublished work.

The slippery quality of race itself emerged during the construction of the series. One of the short novels originally intended for inclusion in the series had to be cut when the family of the author protested that the writer was not of African descent. Another case involved Louise Kennedy's sociological study *The Negro Peasant Turns Inward*. The fact that none of the available biographical material on Kennedy specifically mentioned race, combined with some coded criticism in a review in the *Crisis*, convinced editor Sheila Smith McKoy that Kennedy was probably white.

These women, taken together, began to chart the true vitality, and complexity, of the literary tradition that African-American women have generated, using a wide variety of forms. They testify to the fact that the monumental works of Hurston, Larsen, and Fauset, for example, emerged out of a larger cultural context; they were not exceptions or aberrations. Indeed, their contributions to American literature and culture, as this series makes clear, were fundamental not only to the shaping of the African-American tradition but to the American tradition as well.

Henry Louis Gates, Jr.
Jennifer Burton

PUBLISHER'S NOTE

In the *African-American Women Writers, 1910–1940* series, G. K. Hall not only is making available previously neglected works that in many cases have been long out of print, we are also, whenever possible, publishing these works in facsimiles reprinted from their original editions including, when available, reproductions of original title pages, copyright pages, and photographs.

When it was not possible for us to reproduce a complete facsimile edition of a particular work (for example, if the original exists only as a handwritten draft or is too fragile to be reproduced), we have attempted to preserve the essence of the original by resetting the work exactly as it originally appeared. Therefore, any typographical errors, strikeouts, or other anomalies reflect our efforts to give the reader a true sense of the original work.

We trust that these facsimile and reprint editions, together with the new introductory essays, will be both useful and historically enlightening to scholars and students alike.

INTRODUCTION

BY SHEILA SMITH MCKOY

The right of women to vote is another matter. In half of the republic it would send every negro woman to the polls, while the whites would stay at home, it would plunge a land of peace into horrible discord.

The Atlanta Constitution

Agent Pomeroy of the striking shoe makers told a Boston audience this week that on Merrimac Street, Haverhill, between the bridge and the railway depot, there were at least 800 girls whose room rent was paid by men, he was simply repeating a remark common to this city.

The Boston Herald

* * *

Southern papers are often encouraged in the stand they take by Northern journals which not only acquiesce it by silence, but actually adopy—as did "The Boston Herald" in its 'substrain of animism in the negro' discovery.

The American Citizen
Kansas City, MO

You set yourselves down as a lot of carping hypocrites; in fact you cry aloud for the virtue of your women while you seek to destroy the morality of ours. Don't think that your women will remain pure white while you are debauching ours. You sow the seed—the harvest will come in due time.

The Daily Record
Wilmington, NC

These accounts taken from both majority and black presses from the 1890s disclose how the popular discourse of the era characterizes race and gender relations at the turn of the century. Major white presses across the country participated in protraying black people, and most particularly, black women, as specters, the image of amorality and social rupture. Thus spectered in the visceral cultural space where race and gender combine, the black woman is characterized as a phantasm, not disembodied, but imbued with a persistent physicality. At a time when the racialized discourse figured black men as what Ida B. Wells-Barnett describes as moral monsters,[1] black women were figured as carnal monsters, wholly sexualized in the minds of the white majority.

It is out of this misalliance of "race" and gender that black women organized to vindicate themselves. The histories in this volume chronicle both the proliferation of social activism aimed at this vindication and the sense of agency that writing herstory connotes. As a part of this process, Elizabeth Lindsay Davis's *The Story of the Illinois Federation of Colored Women's Clubs* (1922) and Mrs. S. Joe Brown's *The History of the Order of the Eastern Star Among Colored People* (1925) serve as the historical record of black women's activism.[2]

As Davis's history denotes, the clubwomen recognized the contributions of other groups, particularly the National Association for the Advancement of Colored People (NAACP) and the Pan-African Congress. Of particular note was the need to increase support for the Dyer Anti-Lynching Bill, which was introduced in the House of Representatives in 1921. Brown's history also focuses on the significance of these areas of political and social action. In fact, many of the women who were active in the Illinois clubwomen's movement were members of the Order of the Eastern Star.[3] Significantly, both histories begin with specific references to 1893—the colored women's club movement originating in response to the exclusion of black women from the Columbian Exposition of that year and the O.E.S. text opening with reference to a convention address given in that year. What makes 1893 a watershed year for both of these related but separate movements is the pervasiveness of the sexualized image of black women that the clubwomen and the Eastern Stars sought to correct.

The black woman of this era was denigrated; she was imagined as the contradiction of the sexist stereotypes of passivity and asexuality assigned to white women. While white women, the only women who could be characterized as "ladies," were avenged at the mere supposition of "race rape," black girls, regardless of their age, were "outraged"—to use the prevailing euphemism for rape—by white men who did so with impunity because of the persistent physicality assigned to black women.[4] What becomes integral to this misdefinition of black womanhood is the communal definition of the sanctity of white womanhood. In her study *Teaching to Transgress: Education as the Practice of Freedom*, bell hooks articulates this relationship in terms of a framework in which the white "lady" and the black "whore" are maintained.[5] Focusing on the prevalence of physicality as it relates to images of black women, particularly in this era, Paula Giddings describes the situation that makes black women "vulnerable to sexual assault." Not only were black women made responsible for their own denigration, but they were made responsible for the racial assaults leveled at the entire race.[6] As Angela Davis indicates in *Women, Race, and Class*, these representations of the differences between black women and white ladies had historically figured them as opposites.[7]

The context for the oppositional relationship between black and white women, in fact, lies in the racialization of morality. Arising out of what the *Boston Herald* defined as a "substrain of animism in the Negro,"[8] this system displaces the blame for the violation of black women on the specter of the amoral black woman so ingrained in the popular culture. As such, neither the majority nor the black press reported on the outrages perpetrated against black women to vindicate these women. Instead, these outrages served as addenda to stories about "race rapes" involving black men and white women. Too often the atrocities of white men and the innocence of black men were the thrust of such reportage, rather than a call for justice for the "outraged" black woman. Indeed, "outraged" both physically and emotionally, black women were the focus of the black clubwomen's and female Mason's dedication to racial and gender uplift.

Heralded by what Davis describes as a response to a "letter broadcast over this country and England, reflecting on the character and morals of our Women,"[9] the National Federation of Colored Women's Clubs organized in Boston in 1885 and elected Margaret Murray Washington, the Dean of Women at Tuskegee Institute and the wife of Booker T. Washington, as president. The need for action arose from the escalating tensions between the black workers and immigrant European workers, union strikers and strikebreakers, and agitators and opponents of women's suffrage, all of which particularly affected black women, the least employed and least empowered segment of the population. In response to this, black clubwomen met to protest against the prevailing images of black women who were caught in the nexus of this societal disruption.

Owing perhaps to the prevalence of these contested images of black women, the black club movement represented the alliance of several organizations. The first club in the Federation, the Ida B. Wells Club, was originally organized after the Columbian Exposition of 1893, an event in which African-American women were not allowed to participate. It is in response to the ruling of Representative Women of the World to eliminate "amoral" black women from the exhibition that the colored women's club movement has its roots. The women associated with the movement in its earliest stages, including Fannie Barrier Williams, "one of the few black women invited to speak at the exposition," agitated for full participation by black women and confronted the racist and sexist stereotypes of black women.[10] In addition to the July 1895 organizational meeting, the National Federation of Women's Clubs, with which the Illinois Federation claimed affiliation, recognized another organization, the Women's Loyal Union, as being "identically similar."[11] In recognition of this, the two groups merged in July 1896 under the name of the National Association of Colored Women's Clubs (NACW) with Mary Church Terrell, educator, antilynching activist, and cofounder of the Washington Colored Woman's Club, as president. Davis wrote a history of their activities from 1893 through 1923, entitled *Lifting as They Climb*. (Davis's other history is also reprinted in the series, in the volume edited by Sieglinde Lemke.)

True to their mottoes, "Lift as We Climb" and "Loyalty to Women and Justice to Children," the Illinois Federation of

Colored Women's Clubs (IFCWC) was dedicated to racial uplift. In particular, they targeted black women who were in need of assistance in employment, child care, and housing, all needs that were exacerbated by the black migration to the North in the early 1900s. As such, many of the clubwomen, like their white counterparts, were middle-class, educated women who had both the financial resources and leisure time—something that working-class women lacked—to engage in racial uplift. Many of these "race women" were the daughters and spouses of prominent "race men." Others, such as Wells-Barnett and Terrell, were renowned advocates of black and women's rights. They did not all come from positions of relative privilege, however; at least one, Amanda Smith, was born a slave. Many of the clubwomen had been working-class women. Some were the daughters of the privileged, and others—like Davis—were the daughters of "pioneer" settlers in the state. They came toegther from diverse religious and social backgrounds to challenge both the "race" problem and the woman question. In her preface to *The Story of the Illinois Federation*, Davis contextualizes the power of the movement by naming renowned black women who were active on the national level including Harriet Tubman, Victoria Earle Matthews, Frances E. W. Harper, and Mary McCloud Bethune.[12] In the context of redefining the specter of black womanhood, these black women engaged in social, political, and communal intervention in the black community.

Social intervention into the lives of working black women and children was paramount to the Illinois Federation. Davis characterizes this as an effort to reach "every women in every part of the State."[13] After organizing into three district federations, the members of the Illinois Federation actively sought to intervene in every avenue of concern to black women in the state. They opened kindergartens, supported scholarship funds, provided for orphaned and dependant children, founded homes for the aged, stressed interracial coalition, and agitated for universal suffrage. The areas in which they intervened match the historical record of black insurgency and politics. In addressing black women's activism in the war effort, Davis interweaves the individual histories of the clubwomen. Notably, these clubwomen worked to address the existence of classism in the black community, particularly after the 1919 race riots. As such, the story of their activism not only provides a history of the black club-women's experience, but historicizes black women's responses to the racist, sexist, and classist structures of the period.

While the clubwomen acknowledged participation and support from one man, Frederick Douglass, the O.E.S. was created by a father organization, the black Masons, in the tradition of Prince Hall. As Brown indicates, the organization was founded and chartered on August 10, 1874. The declaration, signed by Brother C.B. Case, is the subject of the 1893 address with which Brown begins her history. What occasioned the discussion in 1893 was an address made by Grand Patron Thornton A. Jackson to the second annual conference of the Grand Chapter of the District of Columbia. Within this address, Jackson outlined the establishment of nine chapters of the O.E.S. in major cities: Washington, DC; Philadelphia; Alexandria, Virginia; and Baltimore. Of the original nine chapters, only two remained in 1891 when four additional chapters were established in Baltimore and Washington. It was with these six chapters that Jackson declared the O.E.S. "an independent body."[14] Significantly, the first chapters not directly chartered by Jackson originated in the South, with chapters in North Carolina (1880) and Tennessee (1881). In fact, by 1893 when Jackson declared the O.E.S. "an independent body," eleven chapters existed from coast to coast. It was a pivotal year because of the place of black women in the imagination of white people, especially in the imaginations of white women. With the Columbian Exposition's exclusion of black women that year, it was incumbent upon black clubwomen to distance themselves from the sexualized and amoral beings that whites—regardless of class, gender, or educational background—imagined them to be. Given the fact that the O.E.S. had a twenty-seven-year history by the time of Jackson's address, it is not difficult to understand why 1893 became a focal point of the organization.

Inundated by the sexualized image of black women in the era, the founders of the O.E.S., like their counterparts in the club movement, focused their efforts on providing for women and youth. Unlike the club movement, the O.E.S. was an organization in which sexism threatened to disrupt the activism of the chapters. As Brown relates, the O.E.S. was created "by Master Masons for the protection of their wives, widows, mothers, sisters, and daughters."[15] For many of the Master Masons, however, "protection" translated into patriarchal control. In her speech to the Ninth Biennial Conference, Brown addresses this problem in her references to the antagonism between Mason brethren and the O.E.S. members in Missouri, Washington, Louisiana, and West Virginia. In the case of Missouri, this antagonism resulted in civil litigation. In the context of the struggle to circumvent patriarchal control that threatened the organization, Brown's history emerges as a testimony to the right of the women of the O.E.S. to control themselves.

Brown commemorates the decision to write her history within the history, itself. While she includes a recommendation in the opening pages of *The History of the O.E.S.* that the "Grimké history [be] our official history,"[16] note how Brown's address also contests this:

> I attempted to gather all the information possible with reference to the origin and history of the O.E.S. among Colored people in America and elsewhere.
>
> I have found that there was a published record of the Order among white Americans from the year 1857 when Robt. Morris, its founder, published his first Ritual down to 1912.
>
> I have also found that there is a published record of Free Masonry among Colored Men of North American from the institution of the first Lodge under Prince Hall in 1775, down to 1903 but find no menton whatever of the O.E.S. or any other department of female Masonry among our women.
>
> I therefore began a research . . . .[17]

In her call to separate women's history from that of the "Colored Men" and that of the "white Americans," Brown opens a space in which black female Masonry can be validated.

Traveling across the country and corresponding with O.E.S. chapters in the United States, Canada, and Liberia, Brown's project provided her an opportunity to report on the work of nearly every one of the existing thirty-eight chapters. Their work included founding homes for widows and orphans and establishing youth programs to produce future race men and women. In addition, the O.E.S. was integral in raising funds to provide Masonic halls, which served as much more than meeting places. These lodges often provided social spaces where black people could view films, bowl, and establish office spaces that attested to the "thrift and enterprise on the part of those who made it possible."[18]

Arising out of a social situation in which their race and gender designated their social and moral place, black women mobilized to contest these notions of black femininity. Both the members of the Illinois Federation of Colored Club Women and the O.E.S. changed the complexion of morality through their dedication to black women and racial uplift. These histories serve as a record of their attempt to exorcise from American culture the image of the black woman as a sexual and social specter. The import of these histories, then, lies in the groundwork they laid for subsequent black feminist activism.

NOTES

[1]Ida B. Wells-Barnett, "The Case Stated," in *Afro-American Women Writers 1746–1933*, ed. Ann Allen Shockley (New York: New American Library, 1989), 257.

[2]Perhaps owning to the fact that the O.E.S. was founded and chartered by the Masons, Brown's name is never revealed in the history. The text bears no hint of her given name, although it does reveal that S. Joe Brown was an attorney and a Grand Patron in the Masonic order in the Iowa district.

[3]Both texts include biographical information on their members. The following women were members of both organizations: Julia Lindsay Gibson, Sadie Pritchard Hart, Susan E. Allen, Sadie Lewis Adams, Carrie Lee Hamilton, and Nora F. Taylor. Since the biographies included in the Davis volume focus only on the Illinois clubwomen, the number of women active in both organizations in this state alone suggests that a significant number of women were active in both organizations nationwide.

[4]Black periodicals in particular focused on the outrage of black girls most frequently when publishing articles about lynchings attributed to race "rape" of white women by black men. Even in the black press, then, black women are figured as addenda to the racial and political pawnage of black men and white "ladies."

[5]bell hooks, *Teaching to Transgress: Education as the Practice of Freedom* (New York: Routledge, 1994), 96.

[6]Paula Giddings, *When and Where I Enter* (New York: Bantam, 1984), 81.

[7]Angela Y. Davis, *Women, Race, and Class* (New York: Vintage, 1983), 47–69, especially p. 58.

[8]Quoted in *The American Citizen*, 15 February 1895, 1.3.

[9]Davis, 1.

[10]Giddings, 85.

[11]Elizabeth Lindsay Davis, *The Story of the Illinois Federation of Colored Women's Clubs* (1922), 1.

[12]Davis, iii.

[13]Davis, 3.

[14]Mrs. S. Joe Brown, *The History of the O.E.S. Among Colored People* (Des Moines: Bystander Press, 1925), 16.

[15]Brown, 41.

[16]Brown, 15. Brown does not give specific information on the Grimké history although William Grimshaw wrote *The Official History of Free Masonry Among Colored People of North America* in 1903. Brown may well have been referring to this history, although there are two possible Grimké writers who may have focused on the subject. Archibald Grimké, a Boston attorney, the editor of the *Hub* newspaper (1883–1885), and a consul to Santa Domingo (1894–1898) may have authored such a volume. His brother, Francis, may also have written such a history, although the records at the Schomburg Collection on freemasonry do not substantiate this.

[17] Brown, 30–31.

[18]Brown, 59.

THE STORY

of the

ILLINOIS FEDERATION

of

COLORED WOMEN'S CLUBS

Price $1.50

Motto

Loyalty to Women and Justice to Children

Preface

When the Public was informed that Mrs. Elizabeth Lindsay Davis would edit a volume relating the story of the Club movement of her colored sisters of Illinois, all looked with anxious eyes for its appearence, knowing that it would be difficult to find a worthier chronicler.

Mrs. Davis by association, training and experience is well fitted for such a task. Knowing her as I do, I confidently believe that she and her production will receive the respectful attention that they merit. Mrs. Davis is a product of Illinois, being the daughter of Thomas and Sophia Jane Lindsay, who were pioneers of Peoria, Illinois. She graduated from the Bureau County High School at Princeton, Illinois. As a child she was possessed of an unusual thirst for knowledge and the high standard of scholarship attained by her in school and college was an ocular demonstration of the fact that a Negro child shows no inferiority and that the inferiority that it seems to manifest in after years is due to its dwarfing and benumbing environment. She seems to have been born for service and with her talents highly cultivated, she felt that she should not hide her light under a bushel.

After graduation, she immediately entered upon her chosen profession, that of school teaching, one of the noblest of the professions, for popular Education as James A. Garfield said, "is next to Freedom and Justice, without which freedom and justice cannot be permanently maintained." She taught in Keokuk, Iowa; Louisville, Kentucky; Quincy, Illinois; and New Albany, Indiana and has been a teacher, in a broader sense, ever since she left the school room.

Her educational work has been in the Sabbath School, upon the lecture platform, in fraternal societies, in clubs of various kinds and in the field of politics. In these organizations she has been a powerful agency in moulding society and has helped all those with whom she has come in contact. Her aim has been to promote the welfare and advancement of not only her own people, but all the people.

It has been my good fortune to have known her for a score and a half years and during this acquaintence I have frequently been in her presence. I have seen her in that home ornamented by her queenly bearing and time and time again I have sat under the sound of her voice as she has spoken upon subjects that have occupied public attention and thought. I have been enlightened by her brilliant thoughts and lifted to higher plains of thought and action by her lofty sentiments. She is one of those choice spirits whom God has given to the world to bless society; a slave to principle, she calls no one her Master.

Mrs. Davis has not lived to herself, but on the contrary, has identified herself with all the great movements calculated to advance her racial group and benefit mankind. She was one of the pioneers in the organization of colored women's club throughout the country. When this movement was inauguarated it had in its ranks many exceptionally strong women, women that any race might feel proud of. Let me name a few of them; Mrs. Mary Church Terrell, Mrs. Blanche K. Bruce, Mrs. Josephine Silone Yates, Mrs. Ida B. Wells Barnett, Mrs. Lucy Thurman, Miss Elizabeth C. Carter. Mrs. Booker T. Washington, Mrs. Mary B. Talbert, Miss Hallie Q. Brown, Mrs. Libbie C. Anthony, Mrs. Ida Joyce Jackson, Mrs. Mamie E. Steward, Mrs. Willie Layton, Mrs. Frances E. W. Harper, Mrs. Emma Ransom, Mrs. Mary McCloud Bethune, Miss Cornelia Bowen and others. In this distinguished group Mrs. Elizabeth Lindsay Davis occupied a conspicuous place, a peer with any of them in her interest in and devotion to a great cause; doing a work that shines out even amid the splendor of this brilliant galaxy of noble women.

She was a charter member of the National Association of Colored Women's Clubs, organized in Washington, D. C., in 1896 and served as its National Organizer from 1901 to 1906 and from 1912 to 1916. While she is a National character, she is not without honor where she lives and is best known. Illinois is prolific with strong women. good women, women who have missions, and a will and desire to perform them. Mrs. Davis is in the front rank of women who claim Chicago as their home. She is a member of the following organizations: Chicago League of Women Voters; Women's City, Woman's Aid, Giles Charity, and the Phyllis Wheatley Clubs, the latter of which she has been president for twenty-four years. She was the promoter and founder of the Phyllis Wheatley Home for girls, was its first president and is a life member of the Board of Directors. Had she nothing to her credit and honor other than the promotion and establishment of this Home for girls, she would long live in the hearts of a grateful people. She is active in social affairs and is a member of St. Marks M. E. Church. Indeed, her whole life has been one of service. The highest tribute I can pay to her is that, she is a good woman; the sacrifices she has made, the work she has performed have not been in vain. They have awakened in her own life and in the lives of thousands of others an aroma that has sweetened society—an invisible influence that is potential for good.

I am quite familiar with what my colored sisters of Illinois have done in club work during the past twenty-two years; they have labored against tremendous odds; they have surmounted obstacles from which hearts less strong than theirs would have shrunk; they have plodded on with the patience of the 'man of Oz' for the goal and their efforts have been crowned with the success they so justly deserve. Many of their offices of Love are unpublished; many of their achievements unheralded, but they have labored on until they stand to day a living evidence of what it is possible for good women to accomplish. As a citizen of Illinois, indebted to my sisters for what they have done to make society better and the atmosphere I breathe purer, I am happy to know that the public is to be told the story of the club movement among the colored women of Illinois. Especially so as that story is to be told by such a worthy personage as Mrs. Elizabeth Lindsay Davis, who on account of the part she has played is able to relate it in every detail.

ADELBERT H. ROBERTS

Chicago, Ill., July 17th, 1922

MRS. JULIA FLORIVEL DUNCAN

Mrs. Julia Florivel Duncan is a member of one of the oldest families in the state of Illinois. She has been identified with the State Federation since its birth and has held most of its important offices. As president of the Springfield Colored Woman's Club, she introduced to the Federation, the idea of the "Mother's Chain", in order to stimulate and encourage the highest ideals of motherhood.

Mrs. Duncan is the proud mother of our gallant Col. Otis B. Duncan of the "fighting 8th" regiment.

The Julia Duncan Auxilary of the 8th Regiment has recently been organized at Springield, in her honor, Mr. and Mrs. Duncan celebrated their golden wedding anniversary two years ago.

MRS. J. SNOWDEN PORTER

One of the native citizens of Chicago who has been a leading figure in organized club work, is Mrs. Joanna Snowden Porter. During her career of activity in civic, social and club work, she has successfully held the offices of: officer of the Juvenile Protective Ass'n., treasurer of the Phllis Wheatley Home and numerous others and is now employed in the Recorder's office of the city of Chicago. As president of the Northwestern Federation, she is earnestly trying to gather the widely scattered race women of the West into a strong organization which will mean for them, all the splendid opportunities that the larger groups of other sections of the country are now enjoying

MRS. CELIA WEBB HILL

President of the Julia Gaston Club, Evanston, Illinois, member of the Phyllis Wheatley Club of Chicago, active in civic, social and religious life and a capable, practical and successful business woman.

MRS. MARY L. MARTIN

President of the Old Folks Home Association of East St. Louis, Ill., has been an earnest and capable worker in community betterment. Under her efficient administration, the Old Folks has had a remarkable growth.

MISS JENNIE E. LAWRENCE

Miss Jennie E Lawrence, the daughter of a Presbyterian Minister, was born in Salisbury, N. C. She received her education at Livingston College and Scotia Seminary in her home State and was a teacher for several years before coming to Chicago to enter her chosen field as a trained social service worker. She served very efficiently as Superintendent of the Phyllis Wheatley Home for five years.

Miss Lawrence was a very earnest club worker for a number of years until her health failed her in 1920. She has taken an active part in all local and political affairs, is a member of the People's Movement Club, has recently been appointed as delegate from the Phyllis Wheatley Club to the League of Cook County Clubs for 1922-23 and is at present employed by the Southside Property Owner's Association.

IDA WELLS BARNETT

Ida Wells Barnett, was born in Holly Springs, Miss, and a daughter of James and Lizzie Wells.. She attended the common schools and later the Rust University.. On June 27, 1895 she married Ferchnand Lee Barnett.. For the last 30 years, Mrs. Barnette has been an editor, lecturer, and soci l service worker. She taught school for 7 years in Memphis, Tenn, and resigned from that vocation to become editor and part owner of the Memphis Free Speech..

Mrs.. Barnett has toured the world as a lecturer, gaining a world wide reputation.. She has always been active in social and uplft work and is considered one of the foremost pioneer club women..

MRS. FANNIE MASON

Mrs. Fannie Mason is another of the pioneer workers in Woman's clubdom. She is an ardent religious, civic and club worker and is now the president of one of the largest political organizations in the city. With the assistance of Mrs Gabrilla Knightson Smith and several other women, she founded the Home for Aged and Infirm Colored People in Chicago.

MRS. LOUISE SOLOMON WALLER

Born in Fayetteville, Tennessee, educated at Nashville and has resided in Chicago for a number of years. She is active in church, civic and club affairs, has served as president of the Frederick Douglass Center and is now president of the Çivic League.

MRS. SARAH SHEPPARD

Mrs. Sarah Shepperd of Peoria is one of the leading down-state clubwomen. She has been a member of the federation for a number of years and has held many of its important offices.

As a welfare worker she has become especially prominent in her home town. She is a former president of the Woman's Aid Club and a member of the City Federation of Women's Clubs of Peoria, which includes all clubs regardless of the race, creed or color of their members.

MRS. EUGENIA SOUTHE TYLER

Mrs. Eugenia Southe Tyler is one of the ambitious young women of Chicago who is forging her way ahead in the club world and who has rendered efficient service as secretary, editor and a member of the Ways and Means Committee of several local clubs and both the city and state federations. Mrs. Tyler was born in Peoria, but has resided in Chicago for a number of years.

LIZZIE JANE CRAWLEY,

Mrs. Elizabeth Crawley, Vice-President of the Chicago City Federation, President of the Ideal and the East Side Woman's Clubs and a member of the Board of Directors of the Phyllis Wheatley Home, has for the past two years, wroked untiringly as chairman of the Permanent Club Home Committee to bring about a realization of the vision which she brought to the Federation, the purchasing of a commodious home for the Clubs belonging to the Northern District.

Born in Nelson County, Kentucky, April 2, 1868, and is the daughter of James and Marandy Gore She attended the common schools in Jefferson County, and at an early age located in Louisville, Kentucky. She married Mr. William Curtis, who died on Feb. 11, 1899. Mrs. Crawley came to Chicago in 1903, and on June 8, 1906, she married Mr. Walter Crawley of this city. She has one son, William Curtis. Since coming to Chicago Mrs. Crawley has been very active in social and welfare work. She is chairman of the executive board of the District Federation of Colored Women's Clubs, was past chairman, social improvement department, District Federation, Colored Women's Clubs, and past president, Ideal Women's Club. Mrs. Crawley lives at 529 East 36th street.

MRS. JULIA LINDSAY GIBSON

Juia Lindsay Gibson is the second daughter of the late Thomas H. and Sophia J. Lindsay and the widow of the late Henry C. Gibson. She has been identified with the Illinois Federation since its start and has filled every office in the organization except that of its President, which, although several times offered to her, she has thus far declined to accept. She filled the office of the first President of the Central District Federation with credit and the same effiency that has characterized her work in other fields. She is an earnest Church and Sunday School worker, has served as President of the Woman's Aid, the Social and Art Literary and is a member of the Mutual Aid Clubs and has been especially active in the Household of Ruth and the Eastern Star. In addition she has been a delegate to a number of the meetings of the N. A. C. W.

MRS. CORDELIA WEST

Mrs. Cordelia West formerly of Evanston, Indiana was the organizer of the Chicago Federation. She is president of the Ida B. Wells and several other local clubs and has held almost every office in the State Federation. As an ardent political worker, she deserves more than passing notice for her excellent work in local, state and national campaigns. Mrs. West is a active church member, a loyal friend and a sympathetic helper in time of need. She at present holds a very lucrative position in the Chicago City Hall.

MRS. DESDEMONA SUBLETT

Mrs. Desdemona Sublett is one of the pioneers in Illinois club work. She is an active member of the Civic League of Quinn Chapel, the Board of Managers of the Phyllis Wheatley Home Association and has held many of the most important office in the State federation. At the last meeting she was appointed chairman of the Pioneer Workers.

MRS. EVA ROUSE

Mrs. Eva Rouse is a native of Chatham, Canada, but has lived in Evanston, Illinois for a number of years. She is active in the club life of the city and state. She is president of the Iroquois Community League and has been one of it most earnest workers in promoting the very much needed Community house, where girls can find healthful recreation, christian guidance and protection.

MRS. GERTRUDE MOORE

Mrs. Gertrude Moore, fourth president of the Phyllis Wheatley Home, is one of the conscientious and earnest Chicago members of the State Federation. Under her administration, the Phyllis Wheatley Home enjoyed a period of unparalled prosperity. Her quiet unassuming personality has won and helps her to keep her many friends.

MARY FITZBUTLER WARING, M. D.

Dr. Mary Fitzbutler Waring has been actively connected with the Illinois State Federation for the past twenty years. She has served as Secretary, Statistician, Chairman of Education, Chairman of Health, and Chairman of the Executive Board.

In 1914 the Federation selected her as their choice for National Commissioner of the Lincoln Jubilee and her appointment by Governor Dunne followed. As a member of Frederick Douglass Memorial Board of Trustees at Washington she has been instrumental in raising the State's share of money and through her efforts twenty names of Illinois Club women and clubs are inscribed on the tablet at Washington, D. C.

She is the founder and for many years served as president of the Necessity Club which maintains the Necessity Club Day Nursery at 3518 Dearborn street.

She has served as Chairman of Health and Hygiene of the National Association of Colored Woman since 1911, in 1919 she represented the National Council of Women and served on the Committee on Better Films. In 1918 she spoke at the meeting of the National Council of

Women at the Statler Hotel in Saint Louis on the treatment of colored people in America. In 1920 she w. s appointed as a representative by the National Council of Women to the International Council held in Christina, Norway and visited thirteen European countries with the American delegation.

In war work she did more in Chicago than any other woman to put things over for the Red Cross. She was chairman of the Auxiliary which knitted over 400 sweaters, 260 pairs of socks, over 100 helmets and made many hundreds of garment for the people of devastated Europe. Also organized and directed until the return of all the soldiers. The c nteen composed of twenty-four colored women who wore the regulation uniform.

Dr. Waring met and served all the colored troops passing through Chicago. She served as a member of the Illinois State Committee on the National Council of Defense and the Mayor's Committee of Chicago to welcome returning soldiers.

After the close of the war she was appointed as a National Organizer of Colored Girls in War Camp Community work doing most efficient work in St. Louis, Missouri.

She is a member of the Delta Sigma Theta and affiliated with all group movements for the good of the people.

She graduated in medicine many years ago but has taught in Chicago for the past sixteen years. At present she is teaching in the Wendell Phillips School and is doing post graduate work in the Chicago Medical School from which she will receive a degree this year.

MRS. DAISY RENFRO

Mrs. Daisy Renfro, Corresponding Secretary of the Federation 1921-22 School Teacher and active club wo- of the Southern District.

She is now president of the Carbondale Woman's Club.

MRS. MARGARET WYCHE

M,rs. Wyche, one of the Life members of the Illinois Federation, is president of the State Federation and is a member of several important committees. Mrs. Wyche was especially commended for her splendid service during the World War.

MRS. LOLA Y. DOWNS

Mrs. Lola Y. Downs is the untiring president of the Julia Gaston club of Evanston, Illinois. No woman in the State has been more faithful to the Federation and the local church, civic and club work than she.

DR. FANNIE EMANUEL

Dr. Fannie Emanuel was born in Cincinnati, Ohio, July 31, 1871. On February 28, 1888 she married Wm. Emanuel of New York City, and shortly after located in Chicago.

In 1908 she took a course in social science at theGraham Taylor School of Civics, several years latter attended the Chicago College of Medicine where she graduated in 1915 with the degree of M. D. Dr. Fannie Emanuel is well known in social and medical circles and is a member of the Board of Directors of the Phyllis Wheatley Club.

MRS. EMMA HOWLAND

Mrs. Emma Howland formerly president of the Julia Gaston club of Evanston is another of the sincere woman who have made possible the remarkable success of the Illinois Federation. She takes an active interest in all affairs pertaining to community betterment and is always ready to lend a hand where there is work to be done.

MRS. JULIA FLORIVEL DUNCAN

REV. CELIA PARKER WOOLEY

June 14, 1848—March 9, 1918

Celia Parker was born in Toledo, the daughter of Marcellus Harris and Harriet Marie Parker. Her girlhood was spent at Coldwater, Mich., where she was graduated from the Coldwater Female Seminary and was later married to Dr. J .H. Wooley (December 29, 1868). She moved to Chicago in 1876 and at once became interested in the literary and civic life of the city. On October 21, 1894, she was ordained as a minister in the Unitarian Fellowship at Geneva, Illinois. In 1904 she organized the Frederick Douglas Center.

This story would be incomplete without a tribute of respect and loving appreciation to the memory of that rare and gifted soul who has entered into the realm of eternal silence. She was easily approached, with an ear ever-ready to hear our story of joy or sorrow, hope or despair. She was interested in all our organizations and institutions from our smallest local club to our great N. A. C. W., and was a valued and helpful member of our State Federation.

Our friends are few and far between and the number grows smaller as the years go by. No words are adequate to express our grief for the passing of Mrs. Wooley, one of the truest friends we ever had. The gentle voice is still, the busy hands are folded, the sympathetic heart has ceased to beat, we cannot pierce the hidden folds of the Great Beyond, where her fearless soul is rising to higher planes of progress, but we can and we will keep her memory green in the hearts of a grateful people for whom she labored and endured much, and who are better and stronger because she lived and walked among them.

IRENE GOINS

Born in Quincy, Illinois, and is the daughter of Mr. and Mrs. Sappington, well-known citizens of Quincy,. She attended the common schools of Quincy and Springfield, Illinois. On Dec. 26, 1894, she married Henry Sherman Goins, of Robinson, Illinois. Mrs. Goins and her husband came to Chicago in 1895, and in 1898 she engaged in the millinery business for herself which she conducted successfully until 1898. Since coming to Chicago she has been very active in social and welfare work and was president of the City Federation of Colored Women's Clubs, 1919-1921. From 1918 to 1920 she was in the employ of the U. S. Employment Service and rendered valuable service to the local Red Cross during the World War. Mrs. Goins is a member of the executive board, Illinois League of Women Voters; vice-president, Illinois Federation of Colored Women's Clubs; vice-president Inter-Racial Co-Operative Committee; Executive Board of Women's Trade Unon League. She is well known in social affairs,and resides at 2942 Prairie avenue.

MRS. ELIZA JOHNSON

Mrs. Eliza Johnson was born in Oxford, Miss., but has resided in Chicago for the past twenty-five years. She has been active in all club and civic affairs, the welfare of unfortunate children particularly appealing to her and is one of the most tireless and conscientious workers in the City Federation. Mrs. Johnson has during her club career, held a number of important offices among which are: Third President of and later Chairman of the Board of Directors of the Phyllis Wheatley Home and President of the Necessity Club in which organization she devoted much time to the club's Day Nursery. At present, head of the Louise D. Marshall Auxiliary of the 8th Regiment, organized in June of 1921, she and her co-workers have in the short period of existence of the Auxiliary, raised over $1,000.00.

This sum was used to improve the lighting and to decorate the Armory and to help defray the cost of one hundred and forty-two trees planted along Giles avenue in memory of those heroes of the Regiment who died on the battle fields of France. The success of the recent dedication of Giles avenue (formerly Forest) avenue in memory of Lt. George L. Giles, the only officer of the 8th to give his life for his Country, was largely contributed to by this group of women.

Sixty eight

MRS. MARY BURTON

Mrs Mary Burton of Sparta, Illinois, is one of the very sincere club workers in her community and was one of the leaders in the organization of the Sparta Woman's Club of which she is now president. At the last meeting of the State Federation, Mrs. Burton was appointed chairman of the Mother's Department

MME. BERTHA L. HENSLEY

Madame Bertha L. Hensley was born in Springboro, Warren County, Ohio, and was at an early age noted for her musical talent. She has been for a number of years an active and energetic worker in Chicago civic and club affairs. She was the 2nd president, is a member of the Board of Directors and Chairman of the Tag Day Committee of the Phyllis Wheatley Home. She is also Chaperon of the Elite Social Charity Club. Madame Hensley is particularly interested in juvenile welfare and spends a great deal of her time in caring for unfortunate children in the city courts. As one of the city's leading modistes she has built up a very successful business.

AMANDA SMITH

Amanda Smith was born a slave in Long Green, Maryland, Jan., 23, 1837. She died at Sebring, Fla., Feb., 23, 1915. In the family was thirteen children, of whom seven were born slaves. Their freedom was purchased by their thrifty father who first bought his wife and then his children, one by one, until all were free. Of this large family only one sister remained to to watch with tender solicitude Amanda's declining days.

In early childhood Amanda Smith showed unusual ability. Capable and pious, she soon enlisted in church work and before she had attained to womanhood she became an evangelist. Later in 1883, her wonderful effectiveness as a temperance lecturer brought an invitation form Lady Somerset, England, to which she responded with a promise of a three months season of work under the auspices of the W. C. T. U., of which Lady Somerset was president. Her success in London and Liverpool was so remarkable that instead of a short stay of three months, her service were continued for twelve years preaching the gospel and temperance in England, Ireland, Scotland, India, Japan and Africa. Then she came home to Chicago to give the proceeds of her life work to bless orphan children.

At the age of 60 years, she founded the Amanda Smith Orphan Home by investing $10,000—every cent of her life's savings, leaving herself penniless in her old age. Maintained by her tireless efforts, the work grew, blessed by her prayers, hallowed by her sacrifices and watered by her tears. Through dark and discouraging days, she kept her lonely vigils supported by a faith which never failed.

Finally success came through a reorganization which placed the work under State control and made its permanence assured. Just as the silver lining fringed the clouds which had darkened the years of her devotion to the great work she had ordained, there came the welcomed msesage calling her from labor to reward.

SADIE PRITCHARD HART

Born in Muscatine, Iowa and has lived in Chicago for a number of years. She is a charter member of the State Federation and the Phyllis Wheatley Home and a prominent member of the Order of the Eastern Stars.

MRS. ETHEL McCRACKEN CLEAVES.

The subject of this sketch, Mrs. Ethel McCracken-Cleaves, is a native of Illinois, having been born in Alton; the younger of two girls, Orleans and Ethel McCracken whose parents are the Rev and Mrs. Newton J. McCracken.

When quite young her parents moved to Chicago, where she was educat ed. After her graduation from High School she attended Wilberforce University and upon the completion of her work there taught school in Colconda and Carbondale, Illinois, until her marriage when she returned to Chicago and became a teacher in the public schools of that city

As a club woman, she has been an ardent worker, serving as president of the Young Matron's Culture Club and as assistant recording and recording secretary of both the city and State Federations. Mrs. Mc-Cracken was the organizer of the Annual United Bazaar Committee, which gave annual affairs and donated its proceeds to the Phyllis Wheatley and the Old Folks' Homes. She is also a member of the Phyllis Wheatley and the Volunteer Workers' Clubs.

SUSAN E. ALLEN

The subject of this sketch was born in Galesburg, Ill., on May 26, 1859, and was the only daughter of James and Clarissa (Richardson) Cannon. The Richardsons and two other families were the first settlers of Knox County and organizers of the Methodist Church there. Mrs. Allen was educated for a missionary in the Monmouth schools with the intentions of teaching in foreign fields. She is the mother of 20 children. 12 deceased. Eight have been reared to man and womanhood and educated in the Galesburg schools. She is a prominent pioneer in club work, being president of the Autumn Leaf Club and one of the organizers of the Woman's Progressive Club. She is a ward worker and member of the Republican Club of the county, a strong advocate for the temperance cause and women's suffrage, Past Worthy Matron of Patron Chapter No. 18, O. E. S., and Stewardess of Allen Chapel A. M. E. Church. Mrs. Allen is a pioneer worker in the Illinois State Federation of Colored Women's Clubs and through the efforts of Agnes Moody attended the Federation first in Peoria when Mrs M. J. Jackson was president.

MRS. EMMA PARKER McDOUGAL

Emma Parker, the youngest daughter of the late Josephus and Mary Parker was born in Princeton, Indiana, December 8, 1864. She was educated in the grammer and high schools of Princeton, attended the Teachers' Normal School in 1884 and taught in Monroe City, Indiana, in 1885.

On September 26, 1886, she married Tobias J. McDougal of Chicago. For over thirty years she has been a resident of the beautiful Chicago suburb of Beverly Hills, where she has raised a family of seven children six of whom are living. Left a widow in 1904, she took up the task of educating her family with the result that; Martha Grace, the youngest child is now a competent stenographer and a pupil of the Chicago University of Music; Horace Morgan, is a Senior in the School of Commerce and Administration of the Northwestern University; Elmer, is a Railway Mail Clerk and Lemuel Girrard, is a student of architecture at Armour Institute of Technology.

Mrs. McDougal entered club work about twelve years ago and has served as President of the Ideal Woman's and the Ida B. Wells clubs and was a delegate to the first Constitutional Convention which met at the Congress Hotel. She was on the program of the League of Cook County

Clubs and submitted a paper that was a credit to her Club and the Race. In 1919 she was a delegate to Tuskegee from Chicago and Northern District Federation, where she was appointed Chairman of Transportation for for the State, to the National Convention in Richmond in 1922.

For over thirty years, Mrs. McDougal has been a member of Bethel A. M. E. Church and for a great part of that time served as a Stewardess of the Church

MRS. MARY SMITH

Mrs. Mary Smith, president of the Study Club composed of a group of young college women, who specialize in research work in Drama and Literature, is one of the younger set of the women's club world. Mrs. Smith has been invaluable as a worker among women and children for the Urban League and has been recently appointed as a visiting teacher by the Board of Education of Chicago. She is the first colored woman to hold such a position and those who know her have no doubt that she will reflect credit upon herself and her race.

MRS. ELLA G. BERRY

Mrs. Ella G. Berry was born in Stanford, Kentucky, but spent the earlier art of her life in Louisville, where she received her common and high school education. Since coming to Chicago Mrs. Berry has been active in club, fraternal and church work and very few women are better known in political circles.

She has been a member of the Cornell Charity Club since 1913, and has been untiring in her efforts to promote the work of the City and State Federations.

Mrs. Berry was always very pronounced in her suffragist tendencies and even before votes were given to women, she was an earnest student of political economy and seemingly graduated with honors about the time of the emancipation of her sex. Among the important positions that she has held, in the field of political endeavor are: State organizer of Hughes Colored women's clubs for the National Republican Headquarters in 1919; investigator for the Commission on Race Relations, appointed by ex-Gov.

Lowden; Federal Census Enumerator in 1920, and president of the Woman's Second Ward Protective League, an organization which has for its objects the strengthening of politics in the Ward, charity and Juvenile welfare.

She has recently been appointed as Home Visitor in the Department of Public Welfare, which gives her the enviable distinction of being the first Colored person to hold a position in that department.

ANNA C. ANDERSON

Born in Fort Scott, Kansas, May 4, 1886 and attend the common schools in Fort Scott. When 14 years of age, she came to Chicago and for two years attended the South Divsion High School. On June 23, 1903 she married James H. Anderson, of New Orleans, La, who died on August 27, 1920. She has one daughter, Mary Anderson. Mrs Anderson embarked in the Beauty Culture field in 1913 and is having a successful career.. She rendered invaluable aid to the United Charities during the World War; is well known in social and welfare circles and has been President of the American Rose Art Club for the past 2 years, having been a member of the Club for 9 years. Mrs. Anderson resides at 3335 Vernon avenue.

CARRIE S. OTEY

Born inTopeka, Kansas October 28, 1877, and is the dauhter of Jason and Mary Scott. She attended the common schools in Topeka and came to Chicago in 1884, where she has remained ever since She had a natural tendency for designing ladies' wearing apparel, and several years after coming to Chicago she embarked into business for herself as a high-class modiste and gained considerable reputation in that field of endeavor. On March 13, 1913, she married Mr. Frank Otey, of Lynchburg, Va. Mrs. Otey moves constantly in social and welfare circles and rendered valuable aid with theKit and Comfort Club during the World War in conjunction with the local Red Cross. She is a past president and member of the Clara-Jessamine Club, is a member of the Beacon Light Court No 1, K. ofP.; Ladies' Auxiliary, Railroad Men's Club No. 79; has been identified with the Phpllis Wheatley Club for many years and was formerly a member on the advisory board of the Phyllis Wheatley Home for about eight years.

MILDRED A. WILLIAMS,

Born in Jersey County, Illinois, May 18, 1886 and is the daughter of Isaac and Elizabeth Weaks, early settlers of JerseyCounty. She attended the common schools in Jersey County and upon reaching the age of 12 she was taken to Alton, Illinois, where she remained four years. In 1902 she went to Springfield, Illinois, where she lived two years and incidentally became identified with the Sunshine Club, of that city, later becoming its president: In 1904 she came to Chicago to engage in the millinery business for herself, and has remained here ever since. On June 9, 1909,she married Mr. Grant Williams, who also comes from Jersey County, Illinois Mrs. Williams since coming to Chicago has been prominent in social and welfare circles. She did considerable work with the Second Ward Club for the local Red Cross during the World War She is a past president and member of the American Art Rose Club and the Town of Lake Charity Club, is a member of the Truste's Aid Club of the Community Center Church and is chairman of the blind reading room.

MRS. IDA MOSBY TYLER

President of the Volunteer Workers Club, born in Detroit, Michigan, but has resided in Chicago for the past 38 years.

SADIE LEWIS ADAMS

Sadie Lewis Adams, born in Staunton, Va., graduated from the public school of Staunton and Hartshorn College, of Richmond, Va. Served as teacher and secretary of Sunday school of John Wesley M E. Church; also first president of Young People's Lyceum of above church. Teacher in the public school of Staunton until her marriage, June, 1892, to James P. Adams. Devoted first 17 years to the rearing of her children, two girls and a boy, to maturity, then began active club work Moved to Chicago in 1910 and became an active member of St. Thomas E. P. Church. Served as recording secretary of the Dorocas Society and is now president of the Dorcas. Also served as recordi ng secretary for the Woman's Home Missionary Society; is a charter member of the Gaudeamus Charity Club, having served for years as recording secretary and three years as president.; charter members of Clara-Jesomine Club and served for two years as recording secretary; charter member of the Baby Relief Club and then first vice-president; member of the Inter-Racial Cirlcle, whose work was to assist the Amanda Smith School for Girls, located at Harvey, Ill.; a member of the Woman's City Club and an associate member of the Y. W. C. A. and Chicago Urban League; served for several years as treasurer of the building fund for Amanda Smith School for Girls at Harvey, Ill., serving as member of the Inter-Racial Co-Operatives committee of Chicago; also as a member of the Illinois Home and Aid Society Board; was one of the first group of women who served on election boards, Mrs. Adams serving as judge and clerk; also served as school census enumerator for board of education in 1916; attended National Equal Rights League in Washington, 1916, delegate from Alpha Suffrage club, the only delegate from the state of Illinois; served as v-president and secretary of the Alpha Suffrage Club the first suffrage club of Colored women in Chicago; attended the Illinois Equal Suffrage League as delegate from Chicago Federation to two conventions held in Chicago; April, 1922, was elected delegate to the Pan-American Congress National League, Women Voters' Convention held in Baltimore, Md.; was the only Colored delegate from the state of Illinois. Record of Mrs. Adams' war work: First gave her only son to fight for world democracy. He was a bugler in Company "F", 365th Inf., was wounded and gassed; finally honorably discharged; gave three hours each day twice a week for child welfare work at Provident Hospital, weighed and measured the babies and wrote record cards; also gave two hours a day, once a week to register women for war work; for services rendered, received a sleeve band" as a mark of honor from "the women's committee, State Council of Defense;" served on citizen's committe to welcome home the 370th Inf. Regt. (old 8th) from the battlefields of the world's great war in France; also the 365th Regt. when they returned to the United States; is amember of Cornerstone No 82, Order of Eastern Star; Liberty Court No. 44,Order of Calanthe; Maid Marian Foresters and Easter LilyClub. After serving as parliamentarian and first vice-president of Chicago and Northern District Federation of C. W. Clubs was elected president in 1921; also served as chairman of civic department of City Federation; now serving the second term as Chairman of the Civic and Labor committee for the Illinois Federation of Colored Women's Clubs.

MRS. SARAH SCOTT

Mrs. Sarah Scott, 6144 Carpenter street, is the wife of Charles E. Scott, Past Eminent Commander of Godfrey Commandery No. 5. For the past 25 years Mrs. Scott has been a deaconess of the M. E. Church and a prominent worker in the Order of the Eastern Star. For 30 years she has worked in behalf of various welfare and charity clubs and at present is the president of the Ladies' Labor of Love Club. She has built up its membership, made many friends for the club and herself, and so managed affairs that the club furnished all the fittings for the bath room of the Old Folks' Home at 4430 Vincennes avenue.

MATTIE JOHNSON YOUNG

Mrs. Mattie Johnson Young was reared in Mississippi, but went to Memphis, Tenn., when she was old enough to earn her own living and worked there until she moved to Chicago. While living in Memphis, she made many friends among the best people there, by the same earnest effort and thorough manner of doing her work, which enabled her to attain and hold for twenty years, the distinction of being the only colored saleslady ever employed by the firm of Siegal and Cooper of Chicago.

By her tact, impartial courtesy and unfailing good humor she was one of the most successful saleswomen of the hundreds who were employed there. As she was the only colored one on the whole floor, she was herself a demonstration to thousands as to her race's capability and the race owes here a debt of gratitude for what she has done along this line.

Her opportunities for school were meager, but she was determined to learn and she seized every opportunity which came in her way to make up for her defiencies, and she has nobly succeeded. Many an evening after standing all day behind the counter, Miss Johnson ate a hurried supper, got her books and started out again for night school. In this way she kept abreast of the times and her business.

In the same way she has become one of the most zealous members of the Bethesda Baptist Church and has for a number of year served as a member of the Board of Directors of the Phyllis Wheatley Home Association.

After the disruption of the firm of Segiel and Cooper, Mrs. Young became a member of the sales force of the Public Life Insurance Company, with which she is now making an enviable record.

MRS. CLARA JOHNSON

Born in Columbia, Missouri, Past President of the City Federation and the Volunteer Workers Club; Chairman of the Exeeutive Board of the State Federation and President of the Phyllis Wheatley Home. An active earnest worker in all church, civic and social affairs of the City and State.

MRS. GRACE WILSON

Grace Wilson, member of Chicago Union Charity Club, wanted to do real work and went to Chicago School of Civcis and Philanthrophy. She took a course in social work and was assigned to the investigation department of the Negro Fellowship League under Mrs. Ida B. Wells Barnett in the city of Chicago.

She took the examination for matron for the State Training School for Girls at Geneva, Illinois, was certified and appointed, being the first Colored woman to hold a civil service position in that institution. She held that position for two years and then took the policewoman examination for the police department in the city of Chicago. She was ceritfied and appointed and now holds that position and has the honor of being the first Colored woman to receive a civil appointment for such a position in Chicago. She has been given creditable mention by the chief of police for efficiency and has won several medals for shooting, the last one from the Chicago Daily News contest given for the police. Many arrests and convictions are given to her credit, murderers among them. She has many friends and Chicago is proud of her only policewoman.

MRS. FANNIE TURNER

Mrs. Fannie Turner came to Chicago in 1904 and her activity in club work dates from her arrival. She is a charter member of the Ideal Woman's Club and was elected second Vice President of the City Federation in 1909, serving in that capacity until June 9, 1910, when both the president and the first vice president having been called from labor to reward, she served the unexpired term and was elected as president for the balance of 1910 and 1911. During her administration she exerted every effort to build up the Chicago City Federation and before passing out of office was successful in raising its membership to thirty-three clubs. Mrs. Turner's efficiency and interest in club work is amply evidenced by the following list of offices which she has held. Chairman of the Executive Board of the City Fedration (1911), President of the Katie D. Tillman Club (1914-17), Vice Chairman of the Executive Board (1916-17), third Vice President (1917-19 and first Vice President of the State Federation (1918-20), and President of the Ideal Woman's Club (1920). Since entering Illinois club work she has missed only one National, one State and two City Federation meetings and those on account of the many duties mentioned. She has not neglected her home, her husband and her family of thirten children.

MRS. PEARL POWELL

Mrs. Pearl Powell, Murphyboro, Ill., is one of the younger women of the Federation and is now serving as a member of the Ways and means Committee. As president of the Golden Seal Club, she is doing splendid work for the betterment of her community.

MRS. ELLA JOHNSON

Mrs. Ella Johnson is one of the pioneer workers in the fields of organized club activities. She has served for over ten years as the very capable treasurer of the Phyllis Wheatley Woman's club.

MRS. IRENE . MOORE

Mrs. Irene B. Moore, born in Kentucky has, since her residence in Chicago go, become one of the leading figures in local club work. She is at present the very efficient secretary of several large and well known organizations and seems destined to be one of the future leaders in the State federation.

FANNIE BARRIER WILLIAMS

Born in Brockport, N. Y., and married S. Lang Williams. Attended the common schools, Brockport Collegiate Institute, New England Conservatory of Boston, Mass, and the school of Fine Arts, Washington, D. C.

Mrs. Fannie Barrier Williams first come into public notice during the "World's Columbian Exposition." By a surprising display of wit and eloquence she won from the board of Control some recognition of the American Negro in the Exposition.

When it was determined to hold a Council of Representative Women of the World in connection with the Exposition, she was selected as an interesting representative of the colored people. Her address on "The Intellectual Progress of Colored Women" before that body created a profound impression..

In the great "Parliament of Religions" Mrs. Williams was again selected to say something of historic interest on the subject, "What Can Religion Further Do to Advance the Cause of the American Negro?"

The address was delivered before the representatives of the world's great religions and is esteemed as one of the remarkable utterances of that notable occasion. Extracts from this address are to be found in all complete publications of the great "Parliament of Religions.

After the close of the Columbian Exposition, Mrs. Williams received invitations from all parts of the country to deliver her addresses.

The peculiar evidence of her merit as an interesting speaker is the fact that she has always been asked to repeat her addresses in the same places. She has been an especial favorite of the great women's organizations.

She is a member of the Board of Directors of the Phyllis Wheatley club.

MRS. NORA F. TAYLOR

It was Mrs. Nora F. Taylor of Chicago, one of the most widely known Evangelists in the country, who brought to the Federation the idea of creating a fund for the establishment of the Monrovian Mission on the West Coast of Africa.

The raising of funds to carry out this project has been one of the main objectives of the Federation's efforts since the acceptance of Mrs. Taylor's idea and its realization will be an event of the near future.

Mrs. Taylor is always busily engaged in club and fraternal work and has served in many of the highest State offices. She expects, when the Mission is established, to carry her work to Africa.

MINNIE A. COLLINS

Minnie A. Collins, was born in Ohio and has been a resident of Chicago for many years, she is the wife of Robert I. Collins and is well known in club and social circles.

Mrs. Collins s one of the pioneer Club women of Chicago, has been identified with Phyllis Wheatley Club for 20 years, is chairman of the Board of Managers of the Phyllis Wheatley Home and is active in church work.

EVA DEROUSSE-JENIFER

Was born in Kaskaskia, Illinois, the first settlement of the state. Her father, Louis DeRousse, came from Pahis, France, and was one of the factors in the settlement of Illinois. After his death her mother brought the little Eva to Chicago, then a primitive city, where she attended the old Clark Street school. She finished school at Champaign, Ililinois, and was married there. She is the mother of three children and through her efforts they received excellent educations. After the death of her husband she established a hair business in Springfield, Illinois, which grew to be one of the largest in the country, and in which she educated many of our girls, who are now conducting successful business in different parts of the United States. Although leading a strenuous business life she never neglected to assist those who were willing to attempt the same, as her motto has truly been ''Lifting as we Climb.''

Wherever she has lived she has left marks of her devotion to others, and many are blessing her for untiring and unselfish efforts. In 1902 she retired from business and moved to Chicago. She placed her church membership in the Institutional A. M. E. church and was an untiring worker there as well as in club work.

In 1904 she married Dr. John T. Jenifer, historian of the A. M. E.

Church, and went to live in Baltimore, Maryland. She at once saw the need of organization there. She called together a large number of refined, intelligent Christian women and placed the need of community clubs before them. They favored the movement, so that when the National Federation met in Brooklyn, New York, 22 clubs were brought in, the largest number of clubs brought in the Federation at one time. There stands today in the city of Baltimore a monument of her work in the Eva Jenifer Community Home for Girls. By all she is loved and honored for her work she did while there.

In 1910 she and her husband went to Chicago, Illinois, to make their home. Seeing the need of a Y. W. C. A. for our girls there she started the one that is in existence there now, stood at the helm with her knowledge of that work and financed it for two years. God blessed her efforts for it is continuing to grow and do much good. During the late war she was one of the most ardent workers in the Red Cross and Canteen work, also graduating as a Red Cross nurse.

After the death of Dr. Jenifer, she decided in 1919 to make her home in Hot Springs National Park, Arkansas, and spend the remainder of her years in rest and grow flowers and raise chickens. So she built a bungalow on one of the hills of that city, surrounded by the beautiful Ozark mountains. It was not long though before she found that her work was not yet ended, and altho she felt she had reached the top of the hill and was going down on the shady side, she could not resist the temptation to help these struggling people. She put new life in the clubs she found here, organized several more, federated them and was made president of the City Federation. She inspired them to improve an Old Folks' Home property they own and it is now repaired, painted and papered and one of the most beautiful places in Hot Springs.

The court, hearing of her work, made her truant officer over the Colored children of the city, and they saw the morals of the city have been greatly improved thru her efforts. Her unassuming ways and kindly spirit has won for her many friends, and pen cannot tell the many deeds of kindness she done.

MRS. EMMA DE COURLANDER

Mrs. Emma De Courlander, president of the New Method Industrial
Club, is active in fraternal, club
and religious circles.

MRS. MYRA HUNTER REEVES

Mrs. Myra Hunter Reeves, organizer of the Young Matrons Culture
Club, also its presdient for two years
and three months, was secretary of
the Executive Board of the City
Federation and Organizer. At present she is chariman of the Ways and
Means of the Northwestern Federation of Women's Club.

Mrs. Reeves won the diamond ring
in the prize essay contest, and has
done a great deal in the way of co-
operation between the schools and the
community. She is at present connected with the Liberty Life Insurance Company.

MRS. RUTH E. GRIFFETTS

Mrs. Ruth E. Griffetts, president of the Benevolent Worker's Club of Marion. She is one of the very active and successful down-state workers.

LIZZIE HUSTER

Lizzie Huster, secretary of Benevolent Worker's Club, Marion is one of the promising club wo-women of the younger set.

MRS. RUTH STEELE

Mrs. Ruth Steele, president of the Young Married Ladies' Industrial Club; Parliamentarian of the City Federation and a earnest club woman.

VELIA W.ARMSTRONG

Velia Armstrong, born in Toluca, Illinois, February 21, 1897 and is the daughter of Andrew and Gertrude Whitner. She came to Chicago at an early age, where she attended the common schools. On September 10, she married Mr. Rex Armstrong of Knoxville, Tenn. Mrs. Armstrong has a character of sterling excellence and is well known and active in social circles.

She is a past president and member of the East Side Women's Club; is a member of the Ideal Woman's Club; is Chairman of the Charity Department of the Chicago District Federation of Colored Woman's Clubs; is also a member of the Olivet Baptist Church. Mrs. Armstrong resides at 4822 St. Lawrence avenue.

MRS. MELVINA COTTON

Mrs. Melvina Cotton has been an active member of the Civic and Social life of Peoria for a number of years. The Woman's Aid Club was organized in her home and she served for several years as its first President. As one of the trustees of the Community House conducted by the Club, she has given evidence of her business ability. She is one of the most faithful members and earnest supporters of Ward Chapel A. M. E. Church and has done splendid work in the Federation.

FANNIE HALL CLINT

Chapter   Seven

INSTITUTIONS

THE PHYLLIS WHEATLEY HOME

Chicago, Illinois.

The Phyllis Wheatley Home for self-supporting girls purchased in 1913 is the leading and most valuable institution in the State. Occupying a commodious and well built brown stone building at 3256 Rhodes ave, of the Phyllis Wheatley Home Association, an organization that greiw out of the Phyllis Wheatley Club, which established the first home at 3530 Forest avenue in 1908.

The object of the Phyllis Wheatley Home Association is to maintain a home which will solve the problem of the colored girl or woman of good character who come to Chicago for the purpose of advancement, often without relatives, friends or money; to surround them with Christian influences, to elevate the standard of employment and to provide a social or community center.

Group of Phyllis Wheatley Girls

The occupants of the Home come through the Traveller's Aid Society through correspondence, and through the directions of organizations recognizing the reliability of the Home and the advantage of its protection.

There is no endowment fund to support this institution, which fact gives it the unique distinction of being the only institution of its kind that has beenmanaged entirely by race women and supported almost entirely by colored people.

The migration from the South has greatly increased the work of the Home. Its facilities are far from adequate to accomodate the large number of applicants for admission. However, the executive board has, for the past few years, bent all its energies to paying off the balance due on the mortgage and have succeeded in reducing it, on the property valued at $25,000.00, to less than $2,000.00.

THE NECESSITY CLUB DAY NURSERY

Chicago, Illinois

The Necessity Club Day Nursery, 3518 Dearborn street, Chicago, represents the attainment of the goal of the Necessity Club whose members ٦ few years raised over $1,000.00 which was applied on the purchasing and remodeling of the building opened in 1920 as a day nursery under the auspices of the Chicago Day Nursery Association.

THE YATES MEMORIAL HOSPITAL

Cairo, Illinois

The Yates Memorial Hospital, Cairo, was opend in December of 1916 by the Yates Woman's Club which had struggled for over twelve years under the leadership of Mrs. William H. Fields, to establish and maintain, for our race group, an institution that would assure efficient and fair treatment, highly skilled medical service and a congenial environment.

This institution not only meets a great need in Cairo, but receives patients from many of the surrounding towns. Annual tag days, musicals, bazaars, etc., are some of the means by which the Woman's Club is enabled to accept for treatment, every sufferer, whether with or without means to pay for the service rendered.

THE LILLIAN JAMIESON HOME

Decatur, Illinois

The Lillian Jamieson Home was founded by the Big Sisters Club of Decatur, and named in honor of Mrs. Lillian Jamieson while she was serving as president of the State Federation. Its object is to provide a home for girls of that city, who have no relatives or friends and who need to be safeguarded and housed at reasonable rates.

THE WOMAN'S AID CLUB HOME

Danville, Illinois

The Woman's Aid Club House was purchased in 1907 by the Woman's Aid Club to give the Club and its Juvenile auxiliary a permanent place to hold ther meetings. The club house has become a great asset for community betterment and as a recreation center for the young people.

THE IROQUOIS COMMUNITY LEAGUE HOME
Evanston, Illinois

The Iroquois Community League of Evanston has worked long and faithfully, under the efficient leadership of Mrs. Eva Rouse, to meet the need of a recreation center for the girls of their city. The beautiful Iroquois Community Home was contracted for in 1921 and the Club expects to open it when the present tenant's lease expires in 1923.

WOMAN'S AID COMMUNITY CENTER
Peoria, Illinois

Some years ago the Woman's Aid Club purchased a piece of property improved with a nine room house, to be used as a meeting place. They have recently decided to have a Community Center in connection.

HOME FOR AGED AND INFIRM COLORED PEOPLE
Chicago, Illinois

In 1898 seven old people were driven from their temporary home by fire. Mrs. Gabrilla Knighten Smith, Mrs. Fannie Mason, and a few other interested friends took upon themselves the task of caring for these unfortunates and rented a house to shelter them until other arrangements

TWO AGED INMATES

NEW HOME
4430 Vincennes Ave.

OLD HOME
510 Garfield Ave.

One hundred

could be made. Mrs. Bela Morrison, a kindhearted German woman, read of their distress and came to visit them. She was so impressed with their condition that she immediately bought all the food she could get at nearby stores (her visit was on a Sunday), gave Mrs. Smith money to temporarily care for them and later gave a house at 510 Garfield boulevard, to be used as an Old Folk's Home.

Mrs. Fannie Mason, superintended the moving of the old people into their home at two o'clock in the morning when several of the white property owners, who later became staunch friends, objected to colored neighbors. A small group of faithful women carried on the work for a number of years until an association was organized and a board of directors was appointed.

Too much praise cannot be given to those volunteer, pioneer workers who gave unstintedly of their time, scarificing much that the old people might be comfortable.

Having outgrown their old quarters, a larger and more modern home was purchased in 1921 at 4430 Vincennes avenue.

Many clubs contributed annually to the home's support, among the largest of these clubs contributors being the Woman's Aid and the Volunteer Workers. These clubs contributions with donations from the Amateur Minstrels, tag days and an occasional bequest form the means of support for this very worthy of the city's institutions.

LINCOLN COLORED HOME
Springfield, Illinois

The Lincoln Colored Home, founded by Mrs. Eva Monroe, is the oldest and best known institution in the State. The Illinois State Federation and many individual club contribute regularly to its support.

THE AMANDA SMITH INDUSTRIAL HOME
Chicago, Illinois   ......

The New Amanda Smith Industrial Home has risen out of the ashes of the old home founded by Amanda Smith at the age of sixty years. Mrs. Eliza Halliday, chairman and former President of the North Side Woman's Club, and her excellent committees are working hard to erect the new building at Harvey during the present year.

One hundred two

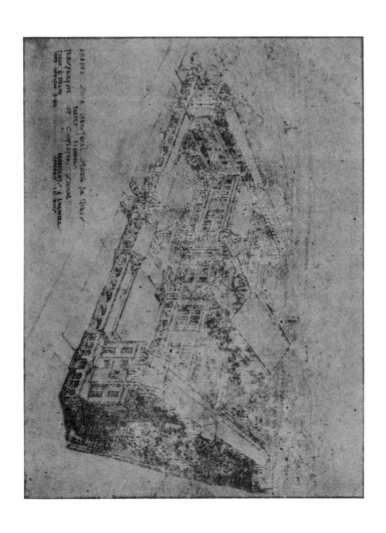

One hundred three

YOUNG MARRIED LADIES INDUSTRIAL CLUB.

Chicago, Illinois

A group of young women who wanted to contribute their little mite toward the uplift of humanity; who wanted to scatter a little sunshine here and there, by helping those less fortunate, on September 14, organized the Young Married Ladies Industrial Club..

They elected Mrs. Ruth Steele as their president and adopted the motto, "Helping Others". The sole object of this club, whch is limited to a membership of thirty, is ch rity and during the six years that they have been organized, over $1200.00 has been raised for the carrying out of their plans.

The presidents of the club have been Mrs. Ruth Steele, Mrs. Arletta Polk, Mrs. Audrey Eberh rt, Mrs. Floyd Edgerton and Mrs. Beatrice Wright. Mrs. Birdie Holoway is the present Secretary.

THE NEW METHOD INDUSTRIAL CLUB

Chicago, Illinois

The New Method Industrial Club was organized in April of 1907 with Mrs. Emma Decoulander as President and Mrs. Minnie Patterson as instructor. This club which has increased from a membership of ten to a limit of fifty-two and has a long waiting list, became affiliated with the city and state federations in 1915.

. Large contributions have been mde to charity and during the war excellent work was done with the National Council of Defense in knitting for the soldiers and in the various drives. The present officers are: Mrs. Laura Yancy, President; Mrs. Mamie Payne, Recording Secretary and. Mrs. Sadie Baskerville, Financial Secretary.

Chapter Eight

LOOKING FORWARD

Twenty two years have passed since our women in Illinois became interested in the work of organized effort.

When we take a retrospective view of the field we are amazed at the marvelous work accomplished in these few short years. We have seen our organization, the first of any of the States to be federated, grew from seven small clubs to more than one hundred throughout the State; seventy-five or more of them banded together in one harmonious effort to be loyal to women and just to children.

There are, of course, in the world of organized effort, two classes of persons—the builders and the wreckers. We are to happy to know and believe that the builders are in the majority. They are the only ones who are ever watchful, ever on the lookout to extend a helping hand to the needy, the suffering and the unfortunate; not for vainglory or self-reward, but in obedience to the divine command. To give a cup of cold water unto the least of these unfortunate ones is giving it unto Him. They are the ones who weekly or monthly, when the doors swing outward, wend their way hopefully to the club meeting, ever ready to join in unity, harmony and co-operation, to further whatever good work is presented for their consideration. They are the ones who support the churches, build homes for the aged, the orphans and the wage-earning girl. They are ever mindful of the child in the slums, the girl in the kitchen, the woman in the alley.

These builders, while ever mindful of affairs philanthropic, are not negligent in matters relative to intellectual and social uplift. We find them thronging our high schools, colleges and university halls, charging the social atmosphere with the strong electric current of their intellectual personality. These builders demand and are getting a better ministry, better school facilities in rural districts, better civic government, better domestic relations, better political opportunities and are convincing those, who will stop to consider, that the world is steadily growing stronger and better in spite of all the new fads, ologies and isms that are springing up everywhere.

The wreckers, although in the minority, are not without their despicable influence; they are the ones who endeavor to tear down what the builders erect. These wreckers do not make good citizens and the greatest calamity that can befall any club is to have one or more wreckers to clog its wheels of progressive activity.

It has, indeed, been gratifying to see our women rising above the frivolities of life, overcoming narrow prejudices, petty jealousies and selfish interests, moving forward to a broader, grander field of noble womanhood and usefulness. We have seen community conditions bettered, improved housing and sanitation, homes established for the aged and infirm, orphans, wage-earning and dependent girls and various other institutions helped, aside from numerous individual charity cases, proving beyond question that five thousand of our women in this State are alive three hundred and sixty-five days in the year, their hearts filled with enthusiasm and inspiration, each doing her level best to make the world better because she has lived.

Not alone at our doors has the work of our women become a recognized factor in the great movements of the world, but everywhere that other races are lending their best forces toward the uplift of humanity, there are we found.

Women "builded" better than they knew when, realizing the value of coming together for mutual help, sympathy and encouragement in a broader, kindlier spirit; they began to organize in groups for community betterment.

Signs of progress everywhere; are as rays of light heralding the dawn of a new day in our history; but it is not yet time for us to fold our hands in quite content, thinking the work so well under way, that we can afford a little breathing space in the rush of world activities. The task is but just begun—the end is far distant—and there is much more to do before we can stand erect and say "Behold the perfect woman.." There is work in the hamlet, village, town and city; there are evils to be corrected, children housed and trained to right living and thinking, young people to be taught quiet manners in public places, habits of honesty, frugality and economy and men and women to be trained in methods of racial unity, harmony and co-operation.

The pulpit and press must join hands with the club women and speak out in loud and no uncertain tones against all things which tend to drag us from the high pedestal of honor, integrity and sterling worth into the mire of corruption, vice and immortality in high places. If we would become strong, we must build from within and not from without; we must respect ourselves if we would demand respect from others.

Women of Illinois, you have done some things well, but greater things remain yet to be done. You have broadened and grown in the past score of years, but there are heights yet to be reached, more difficult problem to be solved, a wider vision of co-operation and unity to attain. ..

We can and do turn our eyes hopefully to the future, which looms up bright with the promise of a better day for all humanity. The National Association for the Advancement of Colored People; the Pan-African Congress recently held in Paris; the increasing sentiment, embodied in the Dyer-Anti lynching Bill, to blot forever from the fair pages of Amercan history, the dark stain of mob violence and lawlessness; the discusson of ways and means of bringing about peace and harmony among all nations and a greater unity of races, are all evidences of our progress.

Appendix

MEETINGS HAVE BEEN HELD AS FOLLOWS:

Chicago, November, 21, 22, 1900; Peoria,; October, 10, 11, 1901 Springfield, August 19, 20, 1902; Evanston, August 18, 20 1903; Jacksonville, October, 11, 14, 1904; Quincy, August 15, 18, 1905; Danville, August, 21, 24 1906; Champaign, June 11, 14, 1907; Bloomington, **October,** Chic go, August, 17, 20, 1909; Peoria, August, 16, 19, 1910; Monmohth, August' 15, 18, 1911; Rock Island, August, 27, 30, 1912; Springfield, Au gust, 19, 22, 1913; Moline, August, 19, 22, 1913; Chicago, August 17, 20, 1915; Champaign, August 29, to September, 1, 1916; Chicago, August, 21, 24, 1917; Bloomington, August 20, 23, 1918; Jacksonville, August, 19, 22, 1919; Galesburgg, August 17, 20, 1920; Carbondale, August 1921; Danville, 1922.

SPECIAL EXECUTIVE BOARD MEETINGS

Chicago, June, 14, 1901; August, 30, 1901; April, 12, 1902; February, 15, 1904; Peoria, and Springfield.

All Executive meetings have since been held at the time of the an- ru l meetings.

OFFICERS:

Officers—1900-1901

Mary J. Jackson, Jacksonvlle	President
Cordelia West, Chicago	First Vice-Preide :
Katherine Tillman, Chicago	econ d Vice Presdent
M. V. Baker, Evanston	Third Vice-Presdent
Julia Gibson, Peoria	Fourth Vice-President
Julia Duncan, Springfield	Fifth Vice-President
Margaret Anderson, Cheiago	Recording Secretary
Jennie C. McClain, Springfield	Assistant Secretary
Mrs. Sarah Floyd, Peori :	Treasurer
E. L. Davis, Chicago	Organizer

Officers—1901-1902

J. C. McClain, Springfield	President
Sarah Reed, Chicago	First Vice-President
Julia Duncan, Springfield	Second Vice-President
R. Yates, Evanston	Third Vice-President
Ella Standford, Peoria	Fourth Vice-President

A. R. Fields, Chicago .... Fifth Vice-President
F. nnie Emanuel, Chic go .... Recording Secretary
Georgia Hall, Peoria .... Assistant Secretary
Mrs. Sadie Allen, Galesburg .... Corresponding Secretary
Margaret Anderson, Chicago .... Treasurer
Sidney Wagner, Peoria .... Organizer
Cordelia West, Chicago .... Chairman Way and Means Comm.

Officers—1902-1903

J. C. McClain, Springfield .... President
Fannie H. Clint, Chicago .... First Vice-President
Julia Gibson, Peoria .... Second Vice President
Mrs. M. V. Baker, Evanston .... Third Vice-President
S. Fields, Chicago .... Fourth Vice-President
Sarah Floyd, Peoria .... Fifth Vice-President
Araminta Davis, Springfield .... Recording Secretary
Blanche Shaw, Chicago .... Assistant Secretary
Elizabeth Fisher, Chicago .... Corresponding Secretary
Mrs. Margaret Anderson, Chicago .... Treasurer
Mrs. Cordelia West, Chicago .... Organizer
Mrs. Julia Duncan, Springfield .... Chairman Ways and Means Comm.

Officers—1904-1905

Mrs. Fannie Hall Clint, Chicago .... President
R. H. Robinson, Danville .... First Vice-President
Emma Smith, Bloomington .... Second Vice-President
Mrs. Fred Dabney, Jacksonville .... Third Vice-President
Mrs. Corinne Knight, Alton .... Fourth Vice-President
Mrs. Annie Wallace, Monmouth .... Fifth Vice-President
Mrs. L. L. Kennebrew, Jacksonville .... Recording Secretary
Lillian Hunt, Chicago .... Assistant Secretary
Mrs. Williams, Aurora .... Corresponding Secretary
Mrs. T. C. Mundy, Quincy .... Organizer
Mrs. E. Baker, Chicago .... Chairman Ways and Means Comm.
Mrs. Ella N. Stanford, Peoria .... Chairman Executive Board

Officers—1905-1906

Mrs. L. L. Kinnebrew, Jacksonville .... President
Mrs. Altheda Moore, Rock Island .... First Vice-President
Mrs. Eliza Holliday, Chicago .... Second Vice-President
Mrs. Marie Toles, Chicago .... Third Vice-President
Mrs. Annie Waldon, Manmouth .... Fourth Vice-President
Mrs. Annie Nichols, Danville .... Fifth Vice-President

Mrs. Bessie Nance .... Recording Secretary
Hattie Morgan, Champaign .... Assistant Secretary
Mrs. Belle Taylor, Rock Island .... Corresponding Secretary
Mrs. Julia Duncan, Springfield .... Treasurer..
Mrs. F. L. Mundy, Quincy .... Organizer
R. H. Robinson, Danville .... Chairman Ways and Means Comm.
Mrs. Annie Peyton, Chicago .... Chairman Executive Board

Officers—1907-1908

Mrs. Annie M. Peyton, Chicago .... President
Mrs. C. O. Lewis, Cairo .... First Vice-President
Mrs. Mittie Foulks, Champaign .... Second Vice-President
Mrs. Emma Waldon, Danville .... Third Vice-President
Mrs. P. F. Denley, Jacksonville .... Fourth Vice-President
Miss L. Pettis, Chicago .... Fifth Vice-President
Mrs. T. G. Macon, Chicago .... Recording Secretary
Jennie Smith, Bloomington .... Assistant Secretary
Miss Clara Webster, ... Corresponding Secretary
Mrs. Julia Duncan, Springfield .... Treasurer
Mrs. Julia Gibson, Peoria .... Chairman Ways and Means Comm.
Mrs. Eva Monroe, Springfield .... Chairman Executive Board
Miss Maggie Wall, Cairo .... Chairman Social Improvement Comm.
E. L. Davis, Chicago .... Organizer
Miss Minnie Hunter, Alton .... Editor

Officers—1908-1909

Mrs. C. B. Knight, Alton .... Chairman Social Improvement
Mrs. T. G. Macon, Chicago .... Organizer
Mrs. William Fields, Cairo .... Editor
Mrs. Eva Monroe, Springfield .... President
Mrs. Mary Clark, Jacksonville .... First Vice-President
Mrs. Ella Stanford, Peoria .... Second Vice-President
Mary DePugh, Evanston .... Third Vice-President
E. Early, Chicago .... Fourth Vice-President
J. B. Bennett, DuQuoin .... Fifth Vice-President
Miss Jennie Smith, Bloomington .... Recording Secretary
Mrs. Annie Buler, Danville .... Assistant Secretary
Mrs. Ella Berry, Chicago .... Corresponding Secretary
Mrs. Carrie Cathey, Danville .... Treasurer
Mrs. Julia Gibson, Peoria .... Chairman Executive Board
Mrs. Maggie Mallory, Jacksonville .... Chairman Ways and Means Comm.

One hundred twelve

Officers—1909-1910

Mrs. Eva Munroe. Springfield .... Presiden
Mrs. Ella Stanford, Peoria .... First Vice President
Mrs. Charlotte Pearson, Chicago .... Second Vice-President
Mrs. Emma S. Kennedy, Chicago .... Third Vice-President
Mrs. Etta Simms, Monmouth .... Fourth Vice-President
Mrfs. Alice Thompson, Moline .... Fifth Vice-President
Mrs. Annie Buler, Danville .... Recording Secretary
Mrs. Tillia Tashley, Bloomington .... Second Recording Secretary
Mrs. Louise Lafayette, Jacksonville .... Corresponding Secretary
Mrs. Carrie Cathey, Danville .... Treasurer
Mrs. Julia Gibson, Peoria .... Chairman Executive Board
Mrs. Maggie Mallory, Jacksonville .... Chairman Way and Means Comm.
Delia T. Carey, Chicago .... Chairman Social Improvement
Mrs. T. G. Macon, Chicago .... Organizer
Mrs. Ella Berry, Chicago .... Editor

Officers—1910-1911

Mrs. E. L. Davis, Chicago .... President
Mrs. S. B. Jones, East Saint Louis .... First Vice-President
Mrs. May Nail, Manmouth .... Second Vice-President
Mrs. Susan B. Allen, Galesburg .... Third Vice-President
Mrs. Della Harrie, Jacksonville .... Fourth Vice-President
Mrs. Altheda Moore, Rock Island .... Fifth Vice-President
Mrs. A. L. Anderson, DuQuoin .... Recording Secretary
Miss Fannie Borhue, Alton .... Second Recording Secretary
Mrs. Collet-Kennie, Milwaukee, Wisconsin, ... Corresponding Secretary
Miss Rosie Hunter, Springfield .... Treasurer
Mrs. Sarah Shepherd, Peoria .... Chairman Executive Board
Mrs. Emma S. Kennedy Chicago .... Chairman Ways and Means
Mrs. Ida D. Lewis, Chicago .... Organizer
Mrs. Eva Jenifer, Chicago .... Chairman Social Improvement
Mrs. Julia Gibson, Peoria .... Statistician
Mrs. Fannie Hall Clint, Chicago .... Editor

Officers—1911-1912

Elizabeth L. Davis, Chicago .... President
Sarah B. Jones, East Sant Louis .... First Vice-President
Mrs. Sarah Niel, Monmouth .... Second Vice-President
Mrs. Susan Allen, Galesburg .... Third Vice-President
Mrs. Della Harris, Jacksonville ....Fourth Vice-President

Mrs. Altheda Moore, Rock Island ....Fifth Vice-President
Mrs. A. L. Anderson, DuQuoin .... Recording Secretary
Miss Fannie Borlun, Alton .... Second Recording Secretary
Mrs. Collett Kinner, Milwaukee, Wis .... Corresponding Secretary
Mrs. Rosie Hunter, Springfield .... Treasurer
Mrs. Emma S. Kennedy, Chicago .... Chairman Way and Means
Mrs. S. C. Shepherd, ... Chirman Executive Board
Mrs. Eva Jenifer, Chicago .... Chairm n Social Improvement Com.
Mrs. Fannie Hall Clint Chicago .... Editor

Officers—1912-1913

Mrs. Ida D. Lewis, Chicago .... President
Mrs. Altheda Moore, Rock Island .... First Vice-President
Mrs. Mary Neil, Monmouth .... Second Vice-President
Mrs. Azalia Taylor, Danville .... Third Vice-President
Violet Newsome, Macomb ....Fifth Vice-President
Mrs. Emma S. Kennedy, Chicago .... Recording Secretary
Mrs. Daisy Lash, Monmouth .... Second Recording Secretary
Mrs. Mary Waring, Chicago .... Corresponding Secretary
Mrs. Rose Hunter, Springfield .... Treasurer
Mrs. Julia Duncan, Springfield .... Chairman Executive Board
Mrs. Belle Taylor, Rock Island .... Chairman Ways and Means
Mrs. Sarah Shepherd, Peoria .... Organizer
Mrs. Julia Gibson, Peoria .... Statistician
Mrs. Hattie Hudln Turner, Chicago .... Editor

Officers Elected

Theresa G. Macon .... 3 years
Elizabeth L. Davis .... 3 years
Eva Monroe .... 3 years
Mrs. Sadie Cooper .... 2 years
Mrs. Nora Taylor .... 2 years
Mrs. Fannie Emanuel .... 1 years
Mrs. Cordelia West .... 1 year

Officers—1913-1914

Mrs. Ida Lewis, Chicago .... President
Mrs. Altheda Moore, Rock Island .... First Vice-President
Mrs. Ella Groff, Monmouth .... Second Vice-President
Mrs. Azalia Taylor, Danville .... Third Vice-President
Mrs. Lillian Reed, Peoria .... Fourth Vice-President
Mrs. Ella Woods, Moline .... Fifth Vice-President

Mrs. Emma S. Kennedy, Chicago .... Recording Secretary
Mrs. Daisy Lash, Monmouth .... Second Recording Secretary
Mrs. Carrie Lee Hamilton, Springfie'd .... Corresponding Secretary
Mrs. T. G. Macon, Chicago .... Fraternal Secretary
Mrs. Julia Gibson, Peoria .... Treasurer
Mrs. Mary F. Waring, Chicago .... Chairman Executive Board
Mrs. Belle Taylor, Rock Island .... Chairman Ways and Means
Mrs. Sarah Shepherd, Peoria .... Organizer
Mrs. Eva Solomon, Galesburg .... Statistician
Mrs. Carrie Hutson, Milwaukee, Wis .... Editor

Officers 1914-1915

Mrs. T. G. Macon, Chicago .... President
Mrs. Sarah Shepherd, Peoria .... First Vice-President
Mrs. Ella Woods, Moline .... Second Vice-President
Mrs. A. L. Anderson, DuQuoin .... Third Vice-President
Mrs. Bessie Kelley, Milwaukee, Wis .... Fourth Vice-President
Mrs. Mary Gostin, Joliet .... Fifth Vice-President
Mrs. Carrie Lee Hamilton, Springfield .... Recording Secretary
Mrs. Adah Davis, Galesburg .... Corresponding Secretary
Mrs. Infelice Thompson, Champaign .... Second Recording Secretary
Mrs. Lulu B. Shreves, Chicago ....Fraternal Secretary
Mrs. Julia Gibson, Peoria .... Treasurer
Mrs. Lillian Jamieson, Champaign .... Chairman Executive Board
Mrs. Etta Simons, Monmouth .... Chairman Ways and Means
Mrs. Cordelia West, Chicago .... Organizer
Mrs. Eva Solomon, Galesburg .... Statistician
Mrs. J. S. Porter, Chicago .... Editor
Mrs. Julia Duncan, Springfield .... Chaplain

Officers—1915-1916

Mrs. T. G. Macon, Chicago .... President
Mrs. Sarah Shepherd, Peoria .... First Vice-President
Mrs. Ella Woods, Moline .... Second Vice-President
Mrs. A. L. Anderson, DuQuoin .... Third Vice-President
Mrs. Hessie Kelley, Milwaukee, Wis .... Fourth Vice-President
Mrs. Mary Gaston, Joliet .... Fifth Vice-President
Mrs. Carrie Lee Hamilton, Springfield .... Recording Secretary
Mrs. Infelice Thompson, Champaign .... Second Recording Secretary
Mrs. Adah Davis, Galesburg .... Corresponding Secretary
Mrs. Julia Gibson, Peoria .... Treasurer
Mrs. Lillia Jamieson, Champaign .... Chairman Executive Board
Mrs. Etta Simons, Monmouth .... Chairman Ways and Means
Mrs. Cordelia West, Chicago .... Organizer

Mrs. Regina Houston .... Statistician
Mrs. J. S. Porter .... Editor
Mrs. Elizabeth Morgan, Springfield .... Chaplain
Mrs. Ella Berry, Chicago .... Parliamentarian

Officers—1916-1917

Mrs. Carrie Lee Hamilton, Springfield .... President
Mrs. Ella Woods, Moline .... First Vice-President
Mrs. A. L. Anderson, DuQuoin .... Second Vice-President
Mrs. Rebecca Logan, Milwaukee, Wis .... Third Vice-President
Mrs. Mary Donnelly, Rockford .... Fourth Vice-President
Mrs. Carrie Drewing, ... Fifth Vice-President
Mrs. Hattie Wells, Champaign .... Recording Secretary
Mrs. Susie Wallace, Springfield .... Second Recording Secretary
Mrs. Frances Morton, Aurora .... Corresponding Secretary
Mrs. Ann a Gillis. Alton .... Fraternal Secretary
Mrs. Mary F. Waring, Chicago .... Treasurer
Mrs. Fannie Turner, Chicago .... Chairman ExecutiveBoard
Mrs. Gertrude Davis, Chicago .... Chairman Ways and Means
Mrs. Ella Stone .... Vice Chairman Executive Board
Mrs. Lillian Jamieson, Champaign .... Organizer
Mrs. Reginia Houston .... Statistician
Mrs. M. Watkins, Galesburg .... Editor
Mrs. Elzabeth Morgan, Springfield .... Chaplain
Mrs. Ella G. Berry, Chicago .... Parliamentarian

L   Officers—1917-1918

Mrs. Carrie Lee Hamilton, Mounds .... President
Mrs. A. L. Henderson, DuQuoin .... First Vice-President
Mrs. Rebecca Logan, Milwaukee, Wis .... Second Vice-President
Mrs. Fannie Turner, Chicago .... Third Vice-President
Mrs. Annie B. Dorsey, Lovejoy .... Fourth Vice-President
Mrs. Milinda Smith, Bloomington .... Fifth Vice-Presdent
Mrs. Carrie Horton, Chicago .... Recording Secretary
Mrs. Susie Wallace, Springfield .... Second Recording Secretary
Mrs. Frances Morton, Aurora .... Corresponding Secretary
Mrs. Altheda Moore, Rock Island .... Fraternal Secretary
Mrs. Adah Davis, Galesburg .... Treasurer
Mrs. Musadora Anderson, Chicago .... Chairman Executive Board
Mrs. Ella Stone, Danville ....Vice Chairman Executve Board
Mrs. Fannie Mason, Chicago .... Chairman Way and Means
Mrs. Lillan Jamieson, Peoria .... Organizer
Mrs. Lucy Webster, Chicago .... Statistician
Mrs. Mignon Watkins, Galesburg .... Editor

Mrs. Lola Y. Downs, Evanston .... Chaplain
Mrs. Geneveive Coleman, Chicago .... Paliamentarian

Officers—1918-1919

Mrs. Lillian Jamieson, Peoria .... President
Mrs. Fannie Turner, Chicago .... First Vice-President
Mrs. Annie Dorsey, Lovejoy .... Second Vice-President
Mrs. Margaret Wyche, Blomington .... Third Vice-President
Mrs. Ollie Price, Springfield .... Fourth Vice-President
Mrs. Fannie Mason, Chicago .... Fifth Vice-President
Mrs. Carrie Horton, Chicago .... Recording Secretary
Mrs. Ethel Cleaves, Chicago .... Second Recording Secretary
Mrs. Elvie Stewart, Chicago .... Corresponding Secretary
Mrs. Luella Barksdale, Springfield .... Fraternal Secretary
Mrs. Adah Davis, Galesburg .... Treasurer
Mrs. Musadora Anderson, Chicago .... Chairman Executive Board
Mrs. Sallie McDaniels, Jacksonville .... Vice Chairman Executive Board
Mrs. Luella K. Taylor, Decatur .... Chairman Ways and Means
Mrs. A. L. Anderson, DuQuoin .... Organizer
Mrs. Mary F. Waring, Chicago .... Statistician
Mrs. Mary Windsor, Rock Island .... Editor
Mrs. Lola Davis, Evanston .... Chaplain
Mrs. Cordelia West, Cheago .... Parliamentarian
Mrs. Elizabeth Lindsay Davis, ... Historian

Officers—1919-1920

Mrs. Lillian Jamieson, Peoria .... President
Mrs. Fannie Turner, Chicago .... First Vice-President
Mrs. Annie B. Dorsey, Lovejoy .... Second Vice-President
Mrs. Margaret Wyche, Bloomington .... Third Vice-President
Mrs. Ollie Price, Springfield .... Fourth Vice-President
Mrs. Fannie Mason, Chicago .... Fifth Vice-President
Mrs. Ethel M. Cleaves, Chicago .... Recording Secretary
Mrs. Minnie Roach, Chicago .... Second Recording Secretary
Mrs. Elvie Stewart, Chicago .... Corresponding Secretary
Mrs. Blanche Mallory, Jacksonville .... Fraternal Secretary
Mrs. Ad h Davis, Galesburg .... Treasurer
Mrs. Sallie McDaniels, Jacksonvlle .... Chairman Executive Board
Mrs. Clara Johnson, Chicago ....Vice Chairman Executive Board
Mrs. Luella K. L. Taylor, Decatur .... Chairman Ways and Means
Mrs. A. L. Anderson, DuQuoin .... Organizer
Mrs. Mary F. Waring, Chicago .... Statistician

Mrs. Corinne Greene, Champaign .... Editor

Officers—1920-1921

Miss Edith Stewart, Moline .... First Vice-President
Mrs. Irene Goins, Chicago .... Second Vice-President
Mrs. Ida Muse, Jacksonville .... Third Vice-President
Mrs Kempie Gibson, Rock Island .... Fourth Vice-President
Mrs. Mattie Walker, Springfield .... Fifth Vice-President
Mrs. Minnie Roach, Chicago .... Recording Secretary
Mrs. Mary N. Brown, Monmouth .... Assistant Secretary
Miss Daisy Renfroe, Carbondale .... Corresponding Secretary
Mrs. Lina Henry, Peoria .... Fraternal Secretary
Mrs. Adah Davis, Galesburg .... Treasurer
Mrs. Clara Johnson, Chicago .... Chairman Executive Board
Mrs. Cordelia Brown, Canton ....Vice-Chairman
Mrs. Eva Solomon, Galesburg .... Chairman Ways and Means
Mrs. Elvie Stewart, Chicago .... State Organizer
Mrs. Victora Thomas, Bloomington .... Statistician
Mrs. Mary DePugh, Evanston .... Editor
Mrs. Arzalia Taylor, Danville .... Chaplain
Mrs. Anna B. Dorsey, Lovejoy .... Parliamentarian
Elizabeth Lindsay Davis, Chicago .... Historian

Officers—1921-1922

Mrs. Anne Laurie Anderson DuQuoin .... President
Mrs. Edith Stewart, Moline .... First Vice-President
Mrs. Irene Goins, Chicago .... Second Vice-President
Mrs. Emma Thompson. Carbondale .... Third Vice-President
Mrs. Adelia M. Ross, Rockoford .... Fourth Vice-President
Mrs. Elzabeth Crawley, Chicago .... Fifth Vice-President
Mrs. Minnie Roach, Chicago .... Recording Secretary
Miss Susie Wallace, Springfield .... Assistant Secretary
Miss Daisy Renfro, Carbondale .... Corresponding Secretary
Mrs. Lina Henry, Peoria .... Fraternal Secretary
Mrs. Frances Morton, Aurora .... Treasurer
Mrs. Clara Johnson, Chicago .... Chairman Executive Board
Mrs. Adah Davis, Galesburg .... Vice-Chairman
Mrs. Eva Stewart, Chicago .... State Organizer
Miss Sarah Clark, Mounds .... Statistican
Mrs. Sarah B. Jones, Alton .... Editor
Mrs. Melinda Smith, Bloomington .... Chaplain
Mrs. Anna B. Dorsey, Lovejoy .... Parliamentarian
Mrs. Elizabeth Lindsay Davis, Chicago .... Historian

One hundred eighteen

CONSITUTION AND BY-LAWS

We, the Colored Women of the State of Illinois, feeling the need of organized efforts, and intending to furnish evidence of material, mental and moral progress made by our people, do hereby unite in a State Federation.

ARTICLE I—Name

The name of this organization shall be Illnois Federation of Colored Woman's Clubs.

ARTICLE II—Object

Section 1. To unite the women's clubs of the State and jurisdiction.   LL

Section 2. To encourage the organization of clubs where such organizations do not exist, and where the hepfulness of women's club is needed.

Section 3. To aid the club in becoming more thoroughly acquanted with the various kinds of work that properly comes within the scope of women's clubs.

Section 4. To pledge to the cause of education, the integrity of the home, the interest and support of the best women of every community.

ARTICLE III—Duties

Section 1. The State President shall preside at all conventions of State Federation; enforce order and decorum; decide all questons of order without debate, subject, however, to an appeal to the State Federation. She shall call the Vice-President to the chair during the discussion of any question before the Federation on which she may desire to speak. She shall at each annual convention present her annual report in writing.

Section 2. The Secretary shall have charge of the records, books, and papers, and keep an accurate account of proceedings, keep correctly an account of all club reports and moneys. At each annual convention present her annual report in writing, and the conditon of the Federation. She shall receive all the money due the State Federation, and pay the same over without delay to the State Treasurer, taking her receipt for the same, and keep an exact and true account of the same, draw all vouchers on the State Treasurer for such monys as may be ordered by the Federation. She shall present a report of all financial transactions at the annual convention.

Section 3. The Corresponding Secretary shall read and answer all communications, letters, telegrams, etc., and send out credentials and blanks to clubs.

Section 4. The State Treasurer shall pay all vouchers ordered drawn by the President, when the same have been properly attested by the Financial Secretary and signed by the President. She shall keep all accounts in a proper manner, exhibiting the source and the amount of the receipt and purposes and amounts of disbursements; give a statement of her office and exhibit a certified check at the annual convention, or whatever required to do so by the Federation of Colored Women's Clubs.

L

Section 5. The Chairman of the Executive Board shall issue the call for the Annual Convention at least 30 days before the time for meeting. She shall preside at the executive meetings and co-operate with the President, during a recess of the Federation in all matters pertaining to the good of the Federaton and the uplift of humanity.

Section 6. The State President and four State Officers with representatives of nine different clubs in good standing shall constitute a quorum of the Executive Board. In an emergency the Chairman of the Executive Board shall give ten day's notice to each club for a call of the Executive Meeting.

Section 7. Should a vacancy occur in any office during the recess of the Federation by reason of death, resignation, removal from the Jurisdiction or otherwise, it shall be filled by the State President, whose appointee shall serve for the balance of the term as prescribed by law. Should a vacancy occur in the Presidency, the next ranking Vice-President shall immediately succeed to the office of President and the power of said office shall devolve upon her.

ARTICLE IV

Section 1. All women's clubs organized for work in harmony with the purpose of this Federation holding regular meetings and having a membership of not less than ten, and not organized for social purposes only, shall be eligible to membership in this Federation.

Section 2. Application for membership shall be made to State Organizer on blanks furnished by the Federation, with an admission fee of two ($2.00) dollars

Section 3. Any financial club woman upon the payment of five ($5.00) dollars may become a life woman in the Federation, the membership to be retained as long as she is a financial member in a local club, said member to have all privileges as a regular elected delegate.

Section 4. Any city or district Federation with a membership of ten clubss or more shall be eligible to membership in the State Federation upon the payment of a regular admission fee of two ($2.00) dollars, and entitled to one delegate for every ten clubs.

Section 5. All clubs must make annual reports on report blanks furnished by Federation.

Section 6. All Past Presidents, State Organizers Secretaries, Chairman of Executives Boards, Chairman of Ways and Means, and Treasurers, who still hold membership in a local club shall be entitled to a voice and vote in the Federation.

Section 7. The majority of votes cast by delegates present

necessary to election.

Section 8. The delegates to National Association shall be President, 1st delegates; State Organizer, 2nd delegate; Alternate to 1st delegate, 1st Vice-President; Alternate to 2nd delegate, Chairman of Executive Board; and a delegate for every ten clubs thereafter.

ARTICLE V—Dues

Section 1. The admission of two ($2.00) dollars pad by each club to the Recording Secretary upon application for membership shall be in lieu of dues for the current Federation year.

But an annual due of ten cents per capita for number of members reported shall be be payable on or before the annual meeting of each year.

Section 2. Any club not paying its dues after two notifications of delinquency have been sent, shall at the end of the year be dropped from the membership in the Federation.

Section 3. Any club wishing to be reinstated shall pay up all indebtness. Prior to opening of annual meeting, Corresponding Secretary shall notify all delinquent clubs of their indebtness.

ARTICLE VI—Representation

Section 1. There shall be allowed one representatives for every ten members and a fraction thereof over five.

Section 2. All delegates and alternates to the annual meeting shall be elected by their respective clubs and their credentials forwarded to Recording Secretary at least five days before the annual meeting. Recording Secretary to turn said credentals over to Chairman of Credentials Committee.

Section 3. The votes to be cast by the delegates present. Chairman of Standing Committees.

ARTICLE VII

Section 1. The officers of the Federation shall be a President, five Vice-Presidents, two Recording Secretaries, a Corresponding Secretary, Treasurer, Chairman of Executive Board, Vice-Chairman of Executive Board, Parliamentarian, Charman of Ways and Means, State Organizer, Editor and Statistician, Fraternal Secretary, Chaplain and Historian. Their duties shall be as usually pertain to respective offices.

Section 2. Officers of the Federation shall be elected on Thursday of the annual meeting at 10:30 a. m., by written ballot of the officers of the Federation and delegates representing clubs whch have paid their dues for the ensuing year. Before balloting the roll shall be called by the Recording Secretary. In answering to the roll, delegates shall state whether the annual dues have been paid. Majority votes cast shall be necessary to choice.

Section 3. Officers shall hold office for one year, and until the adjournment of the meeting at which the election is held.

Section 4. Officers shall be eligible for only two successive terms in the same office.   ....

Section 5. A nomination committee shall be appointed by the President.

Section 6. The Executive Board shall be composed of the officers of the Federation, the President and one other delegate from each local club and the Chairman of all standing committees, Past President, Past State Organizer, Past Chairman of Executive Boards, Past Secretary, Past Charman Ways and Means and Treasurer.

Section 7. Standing committees shall be Arts and Crafts, Book and Magazines, Child Welfare, Credentials. Forestry, Juvenile Court, Music, Press, Program, Religion, Social Improvement, Social Hygiene, Transportation, Ways and Means, Civic, Temperance, Pioneer Worker's Fund, Racial Hstory, Education, Printing, Legislation, Advisory, Monrovian Mission Fund and Mother's Department.

ARTICLE VIII—Meetings

Section 1. The annual meeting of the Federation shall be held on the day previous to the annual meeting and at the call of the Chairman of said Board. Fifteen shall consist a quorum.

Section 3. To secure suitable arrangements for each annual meeting a local committee from the place of the meeting shall be chosen to act with Executive Board in arranging for the conduct and interest of the meetng.

Section 4. The Chairman of any committee will not transact any business without first consulting each member of her committee.

Section 5. Bids for printing of proceedings shall be submitted to the Chairman of the Printing Committee for final decisions, and minutes to be turned over to the Recording Secretary after being printed, for distribution and sold for 10 cents per copy. Proceedings to be printed 90 days after annual convention.

ARTICLE IX

Section 1. There shall be no salaried officers, but proper allowances may be made for all necessary expenses such as stationery and circular communications. The railroad fare of the following officers shall be paid to and from annual meeting: President, Secretary, Treasurer, Chairman of Executive Board, Chairman of Ways and Means, State Organizer and Corresponding Secretary.

ARTICLE X

Section 1. Resolutions relating to the policy of the Federation shall be referred to the Executive Board for consideration before action is taken.

Section 2. All past officers shall turn over to the newly elected officers all property belonging to their respective offices immediately after the session. Recorder shall record and complete proceedings of session before delivering property to the new recorder.

Section 3. The Treasurer shall be required to furnish bond for not less than three hundred ($300.00) dollars. Federation shall pay for the execution of said bond.

Section 4. Outgoing Secretary shall furnish the President of the Federation with a list of all clubs in the Federation, with names and addresses of Presidents and Secretaries.

ARTICLE XI

In the conduct of meetings, Robert's Rules of Order shall be the authority of parliamentary procedure.

ARTICLE XII

Constitution may be amended at annual meeting by two-thirds of those present and entitled to vote. Proposed amendments shall be submitted for approval to the Executive Board and if approved notice of will be appended to the call of the annual meeting.

CHRONOLOGICAL RECORDS

1899. October, Illinois Federation of Colored Women's Clubs organized at the Institutional Church, Chicago, Illinois.

1900. November 21st, First meeting held at the Institutional Church, Chicago, Illinois.

1901. Federation affiliated with the N. A. C. W. at Buffalo, the first State Federation to join the National.

Mrs. Agnes Moody elected Vice-President and Mrs. E. L. Davis, elected Organizer of the N. A. C. W.

Mrs. Newman, president of the 14th Congressional District addressed the federation.

Mayor Warner of Peoria, delivered the address of welcome at opening session.

Among the distinguished visitors were: Mesdames Clara Bowman, M. E. Foster and J. E. Frazier of the Jewish Circle and Miss Cornelia Bowen of Mt. Meigs, Ala., the founder of a Boy's Reformatory in that city.

W. H. A. Moore, prominent poet and writer of Chicago, read an illuminating paper on "Uncle Tom's Cabin".

1902. Met in the Senate Chamber of the State Capital at Springfield. A large delegation of Sangman county teachers was introduced. Greetings were received from the Michigan Federation.

1903. Met at Evanston, entertained by the Julia Gaston Club, one of the "Original Seven". The following named distinguished visitors were present: Mrs. Smith, and Mrs. Lucy Thurman, mother and sister of Bishop S. S. Smith, Detroit, Mich., Mr. Peter Lucky of South America, the Hon. Fred L. McGee of St. Paul, Minn., Mrs. Emma Bradley of Philadelphia, Mrs. M. Coy, Washington, D. C., Mrs. Boone, Rev. Harris, Rev. R. Ranson and Harry Thompson of Chicago, the Misses Ger-

trude and Mattie Fisher of Nashville, Tenn., Mrs. Florence
Lindsay and Mrs. Booth of Ohio.

Letter of greeting received from Mrs. Josephine Silone Yates, of
Kansas City, Mo., expressing regret at her inability to be
present.

1904.   Met at Jacksonville. Unveiling of monument in memory of
Mrs. Mary Jane Jackson, first president of the Federation
Distinguished visitors were; Mrs. Lambert, vice-president of
the Illinois Federation of Woman's Clubs (white) ,who addressed the meeting. Drs. Short and Rogers.

Large delegation attended the N. A. C. W. convention at St. Louis.

1905   Met at Quincy. Many visitors were present among whom may
be mentioned Mrs. Covington of New Mexico and Editor
Thompson of the Des Moines, Iowa, "Bstander".

1906.   Met at Danville. Welcomed by Mayor Lewman. Delegates
visited the Old Soldiers' Home in a body.

1907.   Champaign, Mrs. Daisy Walker, founder of a Home for working girls at Indianapolis, Ind., introduced.

Petitioned President Theodore Roosevelt to stop lynching. Committee
recommended that a annual contribution be given to the
following home; Chicago Home for Aged and Infirm; Yates
Hospital, Cairo; Phyllis Wheatley, Chicago; Old Folks and
Orphans, Sprngifield; Amanda Smith Orphan, Harvey and
the Institutional Church Nursery, Chicago.

1908.   Bloomington. Letter of greeting from Miss Elizabeth Carter
of New Bedford, Mass., president of the N. A. C. W.

Use of colored dolls recommended.

Mrs. Annie Peyton, Chicago, elected Corresponding Secretary
of the N. A. C. W. convention at Brooklyn. Visitors were:
Mr. Thos. Swan of Chicago and Mrs. Craddock, State Editor
of the "Forum."

1909.   Chicago. Address of welcome delivered by Major Franklin A.
Dennison, representing Mayor Busse.

Miss Elizabeth Carter, National President, introduced by Prof.
R. T. Greener, former U. S. Consul to Vladivostok, Siberia.
Reading of colored periodicals recommended.

Mrs. Celia Parker Wooley, founder of the Frederick Douglass
Center; Mrs. McDonald, founder of the Golden Rule Settlement; Mrs. Mathews of the Collegian Institute of Alabama
and Mrs. Susan Lawrence Dana of Springfield, were introduced to the Federation.

1910.   Peoria. Welcomed by Mayor Warner. Greetings received
from Mrs. Preston, president of the Michigan Federation.

Resolution passed to suitably mark the grave of Mrs. Agnes

Moody at Oakwood Cemetery, Chicago.

Judge Clemmons of the Juvenile Court of Peoria, and Mrs Clara T. Bourland of Woman's Club (white) present at the convention.

1911. Monmouth. Welcomed by Mayor W. I. Moore. Madam Partee of the Monmouth Woman's Club, introduced. A Juvenile Department to the Federation was recommended.

Letter sent to the Governor of Oklahoma commending him for an act of clemency to a Negro boy.

The National Association for the Advancement of Colored People was endorsed.

1912. Rock Island. Report received of N. A. C. W. meeting at Hampton Institute. -

Chicago club women attended a reception to Mrs. Booker T. Washington, President of the N. A. C. W. at the Frederick Douglass Center.

Rock Island. Address of welcome delivered by Mayor H. Schriver. The home for dependent girls founded by Mrs. Ida D. Lewis, president of the West Side Woman's Club of Chicago, endorsed.

Mrs. S. D. Brown, representing the "Crisis" and Mrs. Genevieve Coleman, representing the "Fellowship Herald", published at Chicago, urged the women to support both publications.

Rev. Eleanor Gordon addressed the Federation on "Why Women Should Vote."

"Mother Hudlun," one of the oldest club members in the State, was the honored guest of the Federation.

Greetings from California and Boston, Mass., were brought by Miss Marie Simpson and Miss G. W. O'Neal, respectively Demonstrations in the use of "Fireless Cooker" and "Paper Bag" cooking were given by Mrs. Hester Ralls, President of "Koffee Klutch", Chicago.

First Statistical Report prepared by Mrs. Julia Lindsay Gibson of Peoria.

1913. Springfield. Illinois Federation of Colored Women's Clubs, incorporated. Mrs. Sadie Cooper, Chairman of the committee.

Mr. Chas. Clapp, representing the Mayor, delivered the address of welcome on behalf of the City.

Colored Matron recommended for colored girls at Geneva and a committee appointed to visit the school.

Mrs. Blanche. Charleston, president of the Minnesota Federa-

tion, Mrs. Williams, Butte, Mon., Mrs. Jeffries and Mr. More-
land, Secretary of the Y. M. C. A. were introduced. Greet-
ings were received from Mrs. Susan Lawrence Joergen Dahl.
The Illinois Commission on the Half Century of Negro Freedom
Centennial, composed of Bishop Samuel Fallows, president,
Mrs. Susan Lawrence Joergen Dahl, vice-president, Thomas
Wallace Swan, Secretary, Major Geo. W. Ford, treasurer,
Hon. John Dailey of Peoria and Senator T. T. Allain, was
introduced to and endorsed by the Federation. Lincoln Man-
ual Training School endorsed.

Letters of protest sent to each Representative and Senator in
Congress, concerning the alarming increase in discrimination.
Federation adjourned to accept an invitation to visit the beau-
tiful home of Mrs. Dahl.

November 18th, Mrs. Ida D. Lewis, president of the State
Federation passed away.

1914. Moline. A communication received from the North-Eastern
Federation, Miss Elizabeth of New Bedford, Mass., president,
asking the Illinois Federation to join with them in boycotting
all firms and manufactured goods handled by prejudiced
dealers.

Address of welcome delivered by the Mayor. Monument erected to the memory of Mrs. Ida D. Lewis.

A committee appointed to co-operate with the Illinois Commission on the Half Century of Negro Freedom.

Organization of the North-Western Federation recommended.

Prominent visitors were: Mr. Alfred Molief of South Africa and
several others.

1915. Champaign. North-Western Federation Organized. Mrs.
Minnie Scott, president of the Ohio Federation of Colored
Women's Clubs, a visitor.

Recommendation made that the Federation appoint a committee
to appeal to the State Legislature for an appropiation to
build suitable housing quarters for girls who had become
wards of the State.

Dr. Mary F. Waring endorsed as a member of the Illinois Commission on the Half Century of Negro Freedom Centenniel.

Volume of poems written by Miss Bettiola Fortson, a young
club woman of Chicago, endorsed.

1916. Chicago. Alderman Louis B. Anderson delivered address of
welcome on behalf of the City.

Mr. Harmon urged that the women watch the changes to be
made in the Constitution of the State.

The Monrovian Mission a memorial to the colored of America,

which had been endorsed by the Federation, was reported as being finally under construction.

A telegram sent to the President of the U. S. asking his protection of the soldiers involved in the Houston riot until an investigation could be made. A protest against the East St. Louis riot was sent to the Governor of Illinois and the President.

Recommendation made that the departments of Temperance and Child Welfare, be particularly encouraged in every club in the State.

National prohibition endorsed.

1918.   Bloomington. Mr. R. M. O'Connell representative of the Mayor, delivered the address of welcome.

Dr. Mary Waring was appointed trustee of the Douglass Home.

Mrs. Mary B. Talbert, president of the N. A. C. W. reported at the Denver meeting that colored women had subscribed over $5,000,000 to Liberty Bonds.

Mrs. Elizabeth Lindsay Davis appointed as Historian to write the story of the Illinois Federation.

Recommendation made that the Illinois Federation be represented in the Educational Congress at Springfield.

$25.00 donated to the Trustee Board of the Frederick Douglass Home Memorial Fund.

Recommendation made that a short intensive course in military training for boys and girls be made available.

1919.   Jacksonville. Dr. Kennebrew's New Home Sanitarium visited by member of the Federation. Mother's Department created. Bureau of Intelligence created to preserve clippings from newspapers, of articles of race interest. Work of the War Camp Community Service endorsed. Committee appointed to confer with prominent colored men concerning the needs and conditions of the race.

Committee appointed to go to the proper officials to urge the appointment of a Colored Home Visitor in the department of State Welfare.

Recommendation made that heads of departments send a letter once a year to all the clubs, outlining the work to be done in each department.

1920.   Galesburg.   Address of welcome delivered by Mayor Henry Hawkins.

Mrs. Mae C. Green, Mrs. Eliza Logan, Mrs. Margaret Wyche and Mrs. Arzalia Taylor enrolled as the first life members of the Federation.

A handsome flag presented to the Federation by the local G.

A. R. Prof. Zimmerman, a composer of Music, presented to the Federation.

Miss Daisy Renfro, a talented young woman of Carbondale read an original poem.

Mrs. Elnora Gresham, president of the Iowa State Federation of Colored Women's Clubs, a visitor.

Every mother present, led by Mrs. Julia Duncan, the originator of the idea, joined hands to form a circle, the "Mothers' Chain" and repeated an appropriate verse.

Prompt registration of the birth of all babies was urged.

Committee appointed to visit all State prisons. Recommendation made that all clubs urge their members to read race literature.

Federation affiliated with the State League of Women Voters.

1921. Carbondale. Mr. T. B. F. Smith, representing the Mayor, delivered the address of welcome.

Resolution passed denouncing immodest dressing and unchaperoned girls in the "Movies" and other public places.

Corresponding Secretary of the Federation to send a letter of greeting to the Woman's Republican League at Kansas City, Mo., and to request information concerning the organization.

School Lunch demonstration given by Miss Vivian Clarkson of Carbondale, a domestic teacher at Tuskegee Institute.

The Australian Secret Ballot adopted and used for the first time in the election of officers.

Mrs. Easterly, president of the Carbondale Woman's Club (white) and her sister Dr. Colwell, of the Illinois Womans' Voters League gave helpful talks on "Vital Points Pertaining to Politics in Regards to Women".

Recommendation made by the Civics department and adopted, that all clubs establish citizenship classes and organize community and recreation centers.

Resolution adopted urging the organization in every community of committees on inter-racial relations.

A student's scholarship fund established. Federation endorsed the planting of trees in memory of our heroes who fell on the battle-fields of France.

1922. Meeting to be held at Danville. A large delegation from Illinois to attend the N. A. C. W. bienniel at Richmond, Va.

Delegates to N. A. C. W. to attend the dedication of the Frederick Douglass Home, owned by the National, at Washington, D. C., on August 12th.

The names of more than a score of Illinois Clubs and individuals are inscribed on a bronze tablet to be unveiled at this dedication.

THE CLUB WOMAN'S PRAYER.

Keep us O God, from pettiness, let us be large in thought, in word, in deed.

Let us be done with fault-finding and leave off self-seeking.

May we put away pretense and meet each other face to face without self-pity and without prejudice.

May we never be hasty in judgement and always generous.

Let us take time for all things; make us to grow calm serene, gentle.

Teach us to put into action our better impulse, straight forward and unafraid.

Grant that we may realize it is the little things that create differences; that in the big things of life we are one.

And may we strive to touch and know the great common woman's heart of us all, and O Lord God, let us not forget to be kind.

FEDERATION ODE

Written by Katherine D. Tillman

Music by George D. Faulkner

Father in Heaven, we thank Thee
That thus we meet
And in our State Federation
Our sisters' faces greet.

CHORUS:

We women of Illinois
From now throughout all time
Have caught the inspiration
Of lifting as we climb.

Lifting as we climb
Lifting as we climb
We women of Illinois
Are lifting as we climb.

We have tried to carry sunshine
Unto the sad and weak
And for those defenseless
A good strong word to speak.

The old, the young, the erring,
Alike have known our care,
With hearts and hands o'eladed
Our every good to share.

And now we ask Thy blessing.
For all we've tried to do,
Cement our hearts in friendship,
Keep us to duty true!

FEDERATED CLUBS' SONG

By Mary Fitzbutler Waring
Tune: "Baby Mine"

When there's work that must be done,
Illinois, Illinois,
When there's a cause that must be won,
Illinois, Illinois,
To the women's clubs we go,
Where love and charity overflow,
And they never answer "No".
Illinois, Illinois,
And they never answer "No", Illinois.
We must work with utmost zeal,
Illinois, Illinois,
As we have a boundless field,
Illinois, Illinois,
Of things much needed, here,
Of work to be done, here,
And of cries from Everywhere,
Illinois, Illinois,
And of cries from everywhere, Illinois.
To our God who reigns above
Illinois, Illinois,
We give honor, praise and love.
Illinois, Illinois,
For the women of our land,
Who for good and wisdom stand,
In one grand, united band,
Illinois, Illinois,
In one grand, united band, Illinois.

LITERATURE

Federation songs have been written and composed by Katherine D. Tillman, Chicago, set to music by Maggie Mallory, Jacksonville and Mary F. Waring, Chicago, music written by Georgia DeBaptist, Chicago.

PAMPHLETS PUBLISHED

"Some Facts About the N. A. C. W.", Eizabeth Lindsay Davis.

"Racial History," Mrs. A. L. Anderson, DuQuion.

"Health and Hygiene", Mary F. Waring.

"Educational Booklets", Mary F. Waring.

IN MEMORIAM.

These have passed through the veil, and have entered into the presence of their King:

1901—
    Mrs. Mary J. Jackson, First President, Jacksonville.

1902—
    Mrs. Laura Greene, Phyllis Wheatley Club, Chicago.
    Mrs. Maggie Trice, G. O. P. Club, Chicago.

1903—
    Mrs. Agnes Moody, Civic League, Chicago.
    Mrs. Annie Baker, Civic League, Chicago.
    Mrs. Anna Jackson, Civic League, Chicago.
    Mrs. Sallie Emmick, Cornell Charity, Chicago.
    Mrs. Rosa Darnell, G. O. P., Chicago.
    Mrs. Mamie Richardson, Woman's Aid, Peoria.
    Mrs. Emma Haynes, Woman's Aid, Peoria.
    Mrs. Prude Peck, Springfield Club.

1904—
    Mrs. Nora Vires, Woman's Club, Jacksonville.
    Mrs. Henrietta Barnes, Woman's Aid, Peoria.
    Mrs. Ruth Batts, Woman's Aid, Peroia.

1905—
    Mrs. Maltamore, Mother's Union, Chicago.
    Mrs. Randolph, Mother's Union, Chicago.
    Mrs. Banks, Mother's Union, Chicago
    Mrs. Louisa Smith, North Side Woman's Club, Chicago.
    Mrs. Fannie Covington, Woman's Club, Jacksonville.
    Mrs. Phenella White, Woman's Loyal Legion, Quincy.

1906—
    Mrs. Bass, Woman's Aid, Danville.
    Mrs. Jackson, Champaign.
    Mrs. Jones, Urbana.
    Mrs. Catlin, Monmouth.
    Mrs. Ford, Mother's Union, Chicago.
    Mrs. Gill, Mother's Union, Chicago.
    Mrs. Mollie Wilson, Mother's Union, Chicago.
    Mrs. M. M. Roundtree, Jacksonville.
    Mrs. Rawlings, Jacksonville.
    Mrs. Anna Gibbsons Burns, Peoria.

1907—
    Mrs. Transue, North Side Woman's Club, Chicago
    Mrs. Pope, Civic League, Chicago
    Miss Margaret Lee, Champaign and Urbana Club.

One hundred thirty two

Miss Bolden, Champaign and Urbana Club.
Mrs. Anna C.. Parker, Springfied Woman's Club.
Mrs. Grace Mallory, Wednesday Art Club, Jacksonville.
Mrs. Fennoy, Colored Woman's Aid, Danville.
1908—
Mrs. Anna Harris, Springfield Woman's Club.
Mrs. Hattie Hughes, Mary Church Terrell Club, Cairo.
Miss Pearl Wise, Mary Church Terrell. Club, Cairo.
Mrs. Missouri McCreary, Woman's Club, Bloomington.
Mrs. Avery Colored Woman's Club. Danville.
Mrs. Carrie Vance, Woman's Club Danville.
Mrs. Bass, Woman's Aid Club, Danville.
1909—
Mrs. Jane Gray, I. B. W. Club, Chicago.
Mrs. Lizzie Cooper, K. D. Tillman Club, Chicago.
Mrs. Ella Naylor, Springfield Woman's Club.
Mrs. Alice Augustus, Cornell Charity Club, Chicago.
Mrs. Rosa Lucus, Dearborn Center Club, Chicago.
Mrs. Mamie Taylor, Woman's Aid, Peoria.
Mrs. Bell Bannister, Woman's Aid Club, Peoria.
Mrs. Helen Murphy, Civic League, Chicago.
Mrs. Lou Ellston, Phyllis Wheatley, Chicago.
Mrs. Sarah Thomas, Woman's Aid, Danville.
Mrs. Rosa Rummage, Mother's Union, Chicago.
Mrs. Sallie Williams, Woman's Club, Jacksonville.
1910—   I
Mrs. Anna M. Peyton, ex-President, State Federation, Chicago.
Mrs. Irene Camp, Cornell Charity Club, Chicago.
Mrs. Mamie Dunn, Cornell Charity Club, Chicago.
Mrs. Lucy Jenkins, H. Q. Brown, Club, Moline.
Mrs. Laura Jones, Woman's Improvement Club, Milwaukee, Wis..
Mrs. Laura Baxter, H. Q. Brown Club, DuQuoin.
Mrs. Jennie E. Moore, H. Q. Brown Club, Chicago.
1911—
Mrs. Calloway, Woman's Aid, Peoria.
Mrs. Evelyn Helms, Woman's Aid, Peoria
Mrs. Mason, Chicago.
Mrs. Anna Carroll, Woman's Civic League, Chicago.
Mrs. Bell Thomas, Phyllis Wheatley, Chicago.
Mrs. Mary Harris, Chicago.
Mrs. Ruth Simons, Chicago.
Mrs. Seames, Chicago.
Miss Gertrude Payne, Monmouth.
Mrs. Lula Richardson, Galesburg.

Mrs. Leóna Outland, Springfield Woman's Club.
Mrs. Ella Watson, Chicago.

1912—

Mrs. Charlotte Pearson, Phyllis Wheatley, Chiacgo.
Mrs. Josephine Jordan, Phyllis Wheatley, Chicago.
Mrs. Cora Barnes, Volunteer Workers, Chicago.
Mrs. Fryerson, Union Charity, Chicago.
Miss Leona Pole, Non Pareil Girl's Chicago.
Mrs. Rosa E. Moore, Cornell Charity, Douglass Center, Chicago.
Mrs. Jula Green, I. B. W. Chicago.
Mrs. Townsend, Civic League, Chicago.
Mrs. Martha Perkins, Civic League, Chicago.
Mrs. Calloway, Civic League, Chicago.
Mrs. Elenora F. Early, Civic League, Chicago.
Mrs. Addie Tyler, Ideal Woman's Club Chicago.
Mrs. Green, Ideal Woman's Club, Chicago.
Mrs. Molliard Wayman, Industrial Club, Chicago.
Mrs. Mary Casley, Woman's Improvement Club, Galesburg.
Miss Nancy Brown, Phyllis Wheatley, Club, Chicago.
Mrs. Hattie Clay, Progressive Art Club, Rock Island.
Mrs. Harriet Skinner, Agnes Moody Club, Monmouth.

1913—

Miss Hattie Merriweather, Dearborn Center, Chicago.
Mrs. Jakie Smith, Dearborn Center, Chicago.
Mrs. Coffen, Union Charity Club, Chiccago.
Mrs. E. T. Watts, I. B. W., Chicago.
Mrs. Mary Baines, Hallie Q. Brown Club, Moline
Mrs. Martha Reed,- Woman's Aid Club, Peoria.
Mrs. Effie Wheatley, Woman's Improvement Club, Milwaukee.
Mrs. Jennie Scott, Fine Art Club, Chicago.
Mrs. Jennie Peyton, Fine Art Club, Chicago.
Mrs. Laura Jones, Fine Art Club, Chicago.

1914—

Mrs. Ida D. Lewis, ex-President, State Federation, Chicago.
Mrs. Sallie Foreman, Eureka Fine Arts, Chicago.
Mrs. Maggie Johnson, Woman's Aid, Peoria.
Mrs. Lula Slaughter, Progressive Art, Rock Island.
Mrs. Virginia Shaw, Phyllis Wheatley, Joliet.
Mrs. Mary Richie, Julia Gaston Club, Evanston.
Mrs. Minnie Mitchell, Phyllis Wheatley, Galesburg.
Mrs. Julia Butler, Galesburg.

1915—

Mrs. Georgie Taylor, Cornell Charity Club, Chicago.
Mrs. Sallie Herron, I. B. W., Chicago.

Mrs. Hattie Mitchell, Chicago.
Mrs. Mollie Brown, K. D. Tillman, Chicago.
Mrs. Ella Walkup, President Twin City Embroidery Club.
Mrs. Lucretia Niehs, Big Sisters Club, Decatur.
Mrs. Eva Raymond, Tri City Federation.
Mrs. Cynthia Pierce, Home Economics, Champaign.
Mrs. Morton, Woman's Aid, Peoria.
Mrs. Edna Walton, Alpha Suffrage, Chicago.
Mrs. Thalia S. Raglan, Phyllis Wheatley, Joliet.
Mrs. Sallie Partie, Woman's Club, Danville.
Mrs. Mamie Richardson, Galesburg.
Mrs. Agnes Burres, Progressive Art, Rock Island.
Mrs. Louis Dove, Agnes Moody Club, Monmouth.
Mrs. Nerandia Floyd, Agnes Moody, Monmouth.

1916—
Mrs. Lillan Amos, New Method Industrial Club, Chicago.
Mrs. Sarah Goldhand, West Side Woman's Club, Chicago.
Mrs. Tusa Burton, Eureka Fine Arts, Club.
Mrs. Lulu L. Robinson, Eleanor Club, Chicago.
Mrs. Helen Collins, Cornell Charity, Chicago.
Mrs. Florence Smith, Cornell No.. 2, Chicago.
Miss Jessie Maud Butler, Fidelis and Silver Leaf Clubs, Chicago.
Mrs. J. A. Jones, Labor and Love, Chicago.
Miss Alberta Francewat, East Side Club, Chicago.
Mrs. Agnes Pennington, Progressive Art, Rock Island.
Miss Lillian Blue, West Side Ladies' Art, Jacksonville.
Mrs. R. Tucker, Tri City Charitable Aid, Cairo.
Mrs. F. Bates, Tri City Charitable Aid, Cairo.

1916—
Mrs. Beulah Thatcher Hall, Neighborhood Club, Cairo.
Mrs. Jessie Jones, Neighborhood Club, Cairo.
Mrs. Joanna Dent, Springfield Woman's Club.
Mrs. Marie Fuqua, Phyllis Wheatley, Joliet.
Mrs. Lena Suttles, Phyllis Wheatley, Joliet.
Mrs. Ida Barton, Phyllis Wheatley, Aurora.

1917—
Mrs. Bell Grady Smith.
Mrs. Lllian Dyer Settles.
Mrs. Rose B. Ardwell.
Mrs. Soula Mason, Hallie Q. Brown Club, DeQuion.
Mrs. Elizabeth Burkshead, MaComb.
Mrs. Jessie Wilson, West Side Womans Club, Chicago.
Mrs. Louise Foster, Cornell Charity Club, Chicago.
Mrs. Clara Studemre, Chairman Board of Directors Phyllis

Wheatley Home.

Mrs. Jessie Taylor Johnson, Phyllis Wheatley Club, Chicago.
Miss Bettiola Forston, Mental Pearls Club, Chicago.
Mrs. Susan Davis, Springfield's Woman's Club.
Mrs. Kate Smith, Sojourner Truth, Bradwood.
Mrs. Allie Barrett, Colored Woman's Club, Danville.
Mrs. Wilkerson, Woman's Aid, Peoria.
Mrs. Allicia Lewis, Woman's Aid, Peoria.
Mrs. Addie Brown, Woman's Aid, Peoria.

1918—   L

Mrs. Mary Prentiss, Civic League, Chicago.
Mrs. Tina Johnson, 37th Precint Cub, Chicago.
Mrs. Carrie Tucker, Eureka Fine Arts, Chicago.
Mrs. Anna Sharp, West Side Woman's Club, Chicago.
Mrs. Ellen Steward, West Side Woman's Club, Chicago.
Mrs. Clara Porter, Volunteer Workers Club, Chicago.
Mrs. Mattie Wright, Volunteer Workers Club, Chicago.
Mrs. Rachel Sanders, Volunteer Workers Club, Chicago.
Mrs. Kansas Hanson, North Side Woman's Club, Chicago.
Mrs. Carrie Jackson, Social Art and Literature.
Mrs. Addie Brown, Socal Art and Literature, Peoria.
Mrs. Mamie Smith, Ladies' Lilac Club, Peoria.
Mrs. Claire Dudley, Ladies' Lilac Club, Peoria.
Mrs. O. A. Hardison Yates, Woman's Club, Cairo.
Miss Leonia Ford, Domestic Art Club, Bloomington.
Mrs. Fannie Robinson, Hallie Q. Brown Club, Moline.
Mrs Cordelia Holmes, Hallie Q. Brown Club, DuQuoin.

1919—

Mrs. Susie Simpson, American Rose Art Club, Chicago.
Mrs. M. Stewart, American Rose Art Club, Chicago.
Mrs. Mary Lewis, West Side Woman's Club, Chicago.
Mrs. Fannie Taylor, West Side Woman's Club, Chicago.
Mrs. P. E. Bunch, Town of Lake, Chicago.
Mrs. Barbara Adams, Community Club, Carbondale.
Mrs. Nelle Luster, Domestic Art Club, Bloomington.
Mrs. Glena Caldwell, Domestic Art Club, Bloomington.
Mrs.Jessie Scroggins, Domestic Art Club, Bloomington.
Mrs. Oneita Grigsby, Domestic Parent-Teachers' Club, Mounds.
Mrs. Ella Allen, Phyllis Wheatley,Galesburg.
Mrs. Mollie Robinson, Hallie Q. Brown, Moln.
Mrs. Fannie Brown, Home Economics Club, Champaign.
Mrs. Arzenia Harrison, Maywood and Oak Park Improvement.
Mrs. Ella Dickerson, Progressive Art, Rock Island, Ill.
Mrs. Melinda Johnson, Woman's Aid, Peoria.

Mrs. Addie Conway, Woman'sAid, Peora.

MissHelen K. Fields, Yates Club; Cairo.

1920—

Mrs. Estella Miller, Young Matron's Culture Club, Chicago.

Mrs. Maud Forbes, Parliamentarian City Federation.

Mrs. Hester Kennedy, Guademus Charity, Chicago.

Mrs. Maud Glover, Autuumn Leaf, Galesburg.

Mrs. Etta Simms, Agnes Moody, Monmouth.

Mrs. Josephine Coluest, Hallie Q. Brown Club, Moline.

Mrs. Belle Smth, Hallie Q. Brown Club, DuQuoin.

Mrs. Lizzie Dement, Hallie. Q. Brown Club, DuBuoin.

Mrs. Cnderella McGruden, Industrial Club, MaComb.

Mrs. Emma McGolden, Cornell Charity Club, Chicago.

Mrs. Musader Anderson, ex-Chairman State Executive Comm.

1921—

Mrs. Lee, Woman's Civic League, Chicago.

Mrs. Margaret Brown, Woman's Civic League, Chicago.

Mrs. Houston Woman's Civic League, Chicago.

Mrs. Patsy Brown, West Side Woman's Club, Chicago.

Mrs. Elnora Hardin, Volunteer Workers, Chicago.

Mrs. Cynthia Yocum, Union Charity, Chicago.

Mrs. Julia Henderson, Town of Lake, Chicago.

Mrs. Mellisa Coleman, Progressive Art, Rock Island.

Mrs. Juda Barnett, West Side Ladies' Art, Jacksonville.

Mrs. Alberta Wheeler, Domestic Art, Bloomington.

Mrs. Emma Morse, Domestc Art, Bloomington.

Mrs. Henrietta Jones, Sunhsine Club, Harrisburg.

Mrs. Barnetta Williams, Young Ladies' Married Industrial, Chicago.

Mrs. Fannie Neal, Yates Woman's Club, Cairo.

Mrs. Lida Tyler, Tr-City Club, Cairo.

Organized Name	Location	President	Corresponding Secretary
1903	Agnes Moody, Monmouth	Mrs. Flood	Lavinia May, 701 S. 6th Street
1909	American Rose Art, Chicago	Mrs. A. Anderson	Mrs. K. Slayton, 4217 Evans Avenue.
1914	Aurora Culture Club, Aurora	Mable Miller	Dora Hunter, 451 Ogden Street.
1913	Art and Study, Moline	Nora B. Brown	Edith May Stewart, 1816 18th Street.
1890	Autumn Leaf, Galesburg	Emma Kidd	Eva Soloman, 1413 Haynor Avenue.
1914	Big Sisters, Decatur	Mamie K. Carr	Carrie Gardner, 1035 W. Cerro Gordo.
1919	Benevolent Workers, Marion	Ruth Griffin	Annie Gaines, 1210 S. Liberty Street.
1918	Community Club, Cartondale	I. B. Thompson	Vivian M. Clarkson, N. Illinois Street.
1921	Colored Woman's Unity Club, Alton	Mamie Lawry	Gertrude E. Day.
1910	Chicago Union Charity, Chicago	Clara Brown	Daisy Sutton, 5130 Wabash Avenue.
1917	Central District Ill. Fed. Col. W. C.	Mildred Farrell	Susie Wallace, 119 N. 8th Street, Springfield.
1906	Chicago and Northern Dist. Ill. Fed	Sadie L. Adams	
1909	Culture Club, Galesburg	Mattie Thompson	Adah Davis, 392 N. West Street.
1902	Cornell Charity Club, Chicago	Elizabeth Thomas	
1900	Colored Woman's Club, Bloomington	Emily Wilson	Sadie Fleming, 1502 Fell Avenue.
1902	Colored Woman's Aid, Danville	Arzella Taylor	Flora Thompon, 1014 Harmon Avenue.
1916	Domestic Art, Bloomington	Alberta Fields	Bertha Hale.
1916	Douglas Parent-Teachers', Mounds	Lettie Spann	Rosie Lindsay.
1912	East Side Woman's, Chicago	Emma Owens	Lena Raymond, 4837 Champlain Avenue.
1920	Golden Seal, Murphysboro	Pearl Powell	Maud Loving, South 3rd Street.
1911	Guadeamus Charity, Chicago	Sadie L. Adams	Sarah Turner, 5316 Wabash Avenue.
1908	Hallie Q. Brown, DuQuoin	E. V. Barnett	Mrs. A. L. Anderson, 113 N. Maple Street.
1904	Hallie Q. Brown, Moline	Mamie Williams	Maud Robinson, 1187 26th Street, A.
1907	Imperial Art, Chicago	Bessie Bell	Anna Teney, 433 E. 45th Place.
1908	Ideal Woman's Club, Chicago	Fannie Turner	Lucy Smart, 530 E. 42nd Place.
1921	Industrial Club, Centralia	Laura Luake	Annie Ferguson
1915	Improvement Club, M'vw'd-Oak Pk	Mabel Simpson	Carrie Weatherspoon,38 Washingt'n Blvd, Oak Pk.
1919	Junior Sunbeam, Marion	Bertha B. Merriweather	Etta May Payton.
1898	Julia Gaston, Evanston	Lola Y. Downs	Carrie Evans.
1907	K. D. Tillman, Chicago	Elizabeth Thomas	Ellen Rodgers, 6119 Ada Street.
	Ladies' Civic and Social Club, R'kford	Josephine Diamond	Blanche DePriest, 531 Indiana Street.
1917	Ladies' Lilac, Peoria	Madeline Booze	Fannie Huston, 214 7th Avenue.
1918	Mary Talbert, Cairo	Ella Jones	Zenobia Singleton, 515 12th Street.
1919	Mothers' Club, DuQucin	Daisy Weaver	Ethel Reddick.
1917	North Shore Iroruois Club, Evanst'n	Eva Rouse	Josephine Witt, 1003 Emerson Street.
1907	Non Parell, Rockford	Minnie Gilbert	Edkir Upstraw, 622 Locmis Street.
1911	Necessity Club, Chicago	Laura V. French	Fannie G. Lawson.
1901	North Side Woman's Club, Chicago	Ella Gaston	Eliza Holliday, 1340 N. Wells Street.

Year	Organization	Leader	Contact
1915	New Method Industrial, Chicago	Laura Yancy	Minnie Patterson, 3818 Langley Avenue
1901	Progressive Art, Rock Island	Edith Stewart	Bell Taylor, 520 20th Avenue.
1911	Home Economic, Champaign	Eliza Maze	Lovie Hankins.
1905	Philharmonic Club, Peoria	Mae Ruff	Mamie Smith.
1911	Phyllis Wheatley, Paris	Bell Butler	Helen Brown, 916 S. Central Avenue.
1896	Phyllis Wheatley, Chicago	Elizabeth L. Davis	Ida Lucas, 6024 Aberdeen Street.
1910	Phyllis Wheatley, Galesburg	Margherite Flemings	Dorothy Smally, 223 Michigan.
1921	Phyllis Art, Danville	Josephine Smith	Fannie Boyden, 622 E. Harrison.
1899	Peoria Woman's Aid, Peoria	Lina Henry	Emma Chavis, 808 Frye Avenue.
1919	Richard Allen, Elkvills	Ella B. Thompson	Bella Claybrook.
1918	Sojurner Truth Club, Ca.bondale	Velma Woods	Varona Shepperd.
1917	Southern Dist. Ill. Fed.	Alice Beatty	L. W. Spann, Mounds.
1919	Silver Leaf, Mounds	Lulu Bo'en	Della Clark.
1899	Spr'gfield Col. Wom. Club, Spr'gfield	Margaret Byrd	Lucile Hill, 1919 E. Stuart Street.
	Social Settlement, Chicago	J. Barbur	
1913	Sojourner Truth, Braidwood	Nancy Johnson	Ada Smith, Braidwood, Ill.
1916	Sunshine Workers, Harrisburg	Lizzie Truitt	Lela Garnett, 622 E. Walnut Street.
1894	Social Art and Literary, Peoria	Julia A. Gibson	Sarah D. Haley.
1916	Thimble Circle, Galesburg	Mary A. Botts	May Catlin Green, 527 W. 1st Street.
1916	Violet Thimble, East Saint Louis	Luaco Gladden	Helen Jackson, 103 N. 14th Street.
1905	Volunteer Workers, Chicago	Lulu Mae Williams	Ida Tyler, 7716 Langley Avenue.
1917	Woman's Club, Br'k'ln, Lovejoy, P. O.	Anna B. Dorsey	Alta Singleton.
1914	West Side Art Club, Jacksonville	Glendora Hill	Mary Johnson, 530 W. Lafayette.
1919	West Side Woman's Club, Bloomingt'n	Lizzie Samuels	Jennie Morris, 208 N. Densmore.
1919	Woman's Club, Sparta	Mary Burton	N. B. Wade.
1913	Woman's Auxiliary, Canton	Nellie Kingcade	Ella May Pickett, Box 484.
1909	Woman's Progressive Club, Galesburg	Mollie W. Crews	Nitta Huff, 560 W. Knox Street.
1913	Old Folk's Home Ass. E. St. Louis	M. L. Martin	I. J. Jones, 1805 Tudor Avenue.
1909	Col. Women's Culture Club, MaComb	Violet Newsome	Garnett McGruder, Cor. E. Marry and Monroe.
1909	Woman's Improvement, Milwaukee	Willie E. Simpson	Josephine Laurie, 311 9th Street.
1917	Woman's Opportunity Club, Mounds	Carrie Rushing	Inez Mosely.
1909	West Side Woman's Club, Chicago	Alice Bundy	May Alves.
1897	Woman's Civic League, Chicago	Lula Wylie	Louise Waller, 3236 Calumet Avenue.
1905	Yates Woman's Club, Cairo	Alice Beatty	Sarah B. Jones, 420 77th Street.
1911	Young Matron's Culture Club, Chicago	Emma J. Andrews	Cora Corneal, 6447 Evans Street.
1915	Young Married Ladies' Ind., Chicago	Ruth Steels	Viola Frazier, 29 W. 51st Street.
	Clara Jassamine Charity, Chicago		
	Col. Woman's Club, Jacksonville	Cordella West	
	Ida B. Well Clurb, Chicago		

MRS. S. JOE BROWN

THE HISTORY

OF THE

ORDER OF THE EASTERN STAR AMONG COLORED PEOPLE

BY

MRS. S. JOE BROWN
MATRON OF THE INTERNATIONAL
CONFERENCE OF GRAND CHAPTERS
OF O.E.S.

———

Illustrated

———

Publilshed at Des Moines, Iowa
March, 1925

THIS HISTORY OF O.E.S. AMONG COLORED
PEOPLE

is

FRATERNALLY DEDICATED

By the Author to her Co-laborers, and those
Sainted pioneers who have made possible

this Record

CONTENTS

FOREWORD

After associating, in a fraternal way, With Sister S. Joe Brown, of Des Moines, Iowa, our International Grand Matron, and having sat and listened attentively to her reading at Pittsburgh, Pa., Aug. 19, 1924, I am firmly of the opinion that Sister Brown, in the accompanying work, has given to the Eastern Star world the result of years of study, travel and research, which in my judgment, is the most complete concise and authentic history of the Order, among our group of any yet presented. It has rightfully been adopted by the International Conference of Grand Chapters as the official history of the Order and all Grand Chapters should accept it and see that it is properly distributed throughout its bounds, as a long desired necessity.

Sister Brown, in giving this history to the Eastern Star world, has no doubt, added more to our universal understanding and unification than any other one agency, and it will redound to her honor and glorification in years to come.

Our prayer is that she may retain her health and youthfulness and for many years to come, adorn and serve the race and Order. We bespeak for this volume ready acceptance and a broad circulation, throughout the Grand Chapters.

J. C. SCOTT,
International Grand Patron

PREFACE

In compliance with a recommendation made in our report to the Ninth Biennial Session of our International Conference of Grand Chapters of the Order of the Eastern Star, that a committee be appointed to publish a brief History of our Order, and out of consideration for the detailed report submitted at this session, the Conference voted to have published said report as the official History of the Order as expressed in the "Foreword" by Bro. J. C. Scott of Texas, who has not only served in that Jurisdiction as Grand Patron the past 30 years, but who also serves as Patron in our International Conference; it is however, with a bit of timidity that I reproduce the report as made at the Conference but by authority of said conference I do this, and in addition thereto I herewith submit other data gathered from various sources from the several Jurisdictions, and otherwise, as a result of which there will be found in this little volume a list of the Jurisdictions for the most part the year and the date of organization, time of annual meeting, tabulated statistics showing number of Chapters and number of members of each Jurisdiction, Grand Matron and Grand Patron serving in 1924 in the United States of America, in Ontario, Canada, and in Liberia, Africa. And by the way of showing some of the most tangible achievements of our Order we also present a few Illustrations such as Widows' and Orphans' Homes, Temples, etc., and a historical sketch of each telling of the part the Order has played in the erection and maintenance of each.

THE AUTHOR

PRINCE HALL,   Founder of Negro Masonry

1784
THE ORIGINAL CHARTER

(Copy)

Know all men by these presents:

Thus were we greeted by the Grand Lodge on the 29th day of September, A.L. 5784, A.D. 1784; and following said Greeting was warrant 459, granted by the Grand Lodge of England, on petition of Prince Hall, Boston Smith, Thomas Sanderson, and several other Masons of Boston, constituting them into a regular Lodge of Free and Accepted Masons.

"To all and every right Worshipful and loving Bretheren we, Thomas Howard, Earl of Effingham, Lord Howard, etc., etc., acting Grand Master under the authority of His Royal Highness, Henry Frederick, Duke of Cumberland, etc., etc., Grand Master of the Most Ancient and Honorable Society of Free and Accepted Masons send Greeting:

"Know ye, that we, at the humble petition of our right trusty and well beloved Brethren, Prince Hall, Boston Smith, Thomas Sanderson and several other Brethren residing in Boston, New England, in North America, do hereby constitute the said Brethren into a regular Lodge of Free and Accepted Masons, under the title or denomination of the Afrcan Lodge to be opened in Boston aforesaid, and do further, at their said petition, hereby appoint the said Prince Hall to be a Master, Boston Smith, Senior Warden, and Thomas Sanderson, Junior Warden, for the opening of the said Lodge, and for such further time only as shall be thought proper by the brethren thereof, it being our will that this, our appointment of the above officers, shall in no wise affect any future election of officers of the Lodge, but that such election shall be regulated agreeable to such by-laws of said Lodge as shall be consistent with the general laws of the society contained in the Book of Constitutions, and we hereby will require you, the said Prince Hall, to take especial care that all and every one of the said Brethren are or have been regularly made Masons, and that they do observe, perform and keep all the rules and orders contained in the Book of Constitutions; and further, that you do, from time to time, cause to be entered in a book kept for the purpose, an account of your proceedings in the Lodge, together with all such rules, orders and regulations, as shall be made for the good government of the same; that in no wise you omit once in every year to send us, or our successor, Grand Master, or to Rowland Holt, Esq., our Deputy Grand Master for the time being, an account in writing of your said proceedings, and copies of all such rules, orders and regulations as shall be made as aforesaid, together with a list of the members of the Lodge, and such a sum of money as may suit the circumstances of the Lodge and reasonably be expected towards the Grand Charity. Moreover, we hereby will and require you, the said Prince Hall, as soon as conveniently may be, to send an account in writing of what may be done by virtue of these presents.

"Given at London, under our hand and seal of Masonry, this 29th day of September, A.L., 5784, A.D. 1784.

       "By the Grand Master's Command.

SEAL

 Witness: "Wm. White, G.S." "R. Holt, D.G.M."

"We, their descendants not only in a Masonic point of view, but in blood as well, standing upon the soil on which they were born, and viewing their play grounds, shall visit the grave of Prince Hall and place our sprig of Acacia thereon.

 "Thomas Thomas, G.M., of Masachusetts."

ORIGIN AND HISTORY OF THE ADOPTIVE RITE IN THE DIST. OF COLUMBIA.

The following is an extract from the Annual Address of Grand Patron Thornton A. Jackson, (33rd degree), delivered at the Second Annual Communication of the Grand Chapter of the District of Columbia and Jurisdiction, on May 23, 1893, which contains an account of the Histroy and Origin of the Adoptive Rite in the District of Columbia. It is republished here for the information of the members of this Order."

At the organization of this Grand Chapter, I informed you that the history and origin of the Eastern Star Degrees in this Juirsdiction would be of some importance to the members of this Grand Chapter and Subordinates. I said that our origin was pure and undisputed. I informed you that on the 10th day of August, 1874, I received the several degrees of the Rite of Adoption, of the Order of the Eastern Star, from Bro. C. B. Case, a Deputy and Agent of Illustrious Robert Maccy, (33rd degree), the Supreme Patron of the Rite of Adoption of the World, and at which time I received from Bro. C. B. Case a letter of authcrity empowering me to establish this Order among our people. I at once proceeded to establish chapters of the Eastren Star in obedience to the authority with which I was invested."

In 1875 and 1876, I established two (2) Chapters at Washington, D. C.; one (1) at Alexandria;in the State cf Virginia; three (3) at Baltimore, in the State of Maryland; and three (at Philadelphia, in the State of Pennsylvania. So you see in the short space of eighteen months we had nine (9) Chapters of the Order, all in a fair working condition. Notwithstanding my authority to establish the Rite, but like the Grand Orient of France, I had each Chapter thus organized, adopted by some regular constituted Masonic Lodge, thereby more closely uniting our Masonic family. These Chapters, like some of cur Masonic Lodges, for a time seemed to carry all before them; so they flourished, but soon their course was run, and to-day, out of the the nine (9), all but two (2), Queen

Esther, No. 1 of Washington, D. C., and Electa, No. 2, of Baltimore, Maryland, is a thing of the past.

Two years ago I established at Washington, D. C., Queen of Sheba and Gethsemane Chapters, and authorized Bro. J. Murry Ralph, of Baltimore, Maryland, to establish at Frederick City Maryland, Queen Esther, and at Baltimore, Maryland, Queen of Sheba Chapters, and according to my former instructions each Chapter has been adopted by a regular Masonic Lodge. Now we have a Grand Chapter with six (6) Subordinates, all in a flourishing condition. We are now an independent body."

MASONIC AND O.E.S. HOME—Marion, Ind.

HISTORY OF THE O.E.S.
AMONG COLORED PEOPLE

In the city of Boston, in the year 1907, an organization styled as a Supreme Grand Chapter of the O.E.S. was formed by a limited number of representatives of our then existing Grand Chapters that felt the need of a closer fraternal relationship, whereby there might be brought about a better interpretation of and more uniformity in the ritualistic work, and in the end to encourage the organization of Chapters, that they might co-operate in the great labors of Masonry, by assisting in and in some respects directing the charities and other work in the cause of human progress.

Mrs. Letitia L. Foy, then of Massachusetts, but now of Newburn, N. C. called this meeting together at the conclusion of which the following officers were elected:

Supreme Grand Royal Matron, Sister Kittie Terrell of the Illinois Jurisdiction; Supreme Grand Royal Patron, Bro. Walden Banks, New England Jurisdiction; Supreme Associate Matron, Sister Viola Hart, Georgia Jurisdiction; Supreme Grand Treasurer, Sister Addie Duffin, Maryland Jurisdiction.

August 21st and 22nd, 1908 the second meeting of this body was held in Chicago, Ill. with fifteen Jurisdictions represented. At this meeting a Constitution and By-Laws Committee appointed at the previous session, reported a constitution and by-laws which were adopted and a collection for stationery in the sum of $3.57 seems to comprise the entire receipts of this session.

August 23—25, 1910 the third session was held at Detriot, Michigan, with eleven Jurisdictions represented. Among the recommendations made at this meeting were: the printing of a ritual; the change of the name from Supreme Grand Chapter to Inter-state Conference of Grand Chapters; and, the fixing of the time of meeting as biennially, and at the same time and place as the International Conference of Knights Templar; also that each Jurisdiction be required to pay a membership fee of two cents per capita and a total of $54 was collected at this meeting.

August 21—22, 1912 the fourth session was held in Washington, D. C., with eleven Jurisdictions again represented and "The Order of the Eastern Star and its development among our People" was a much discussed topic at this meeting after which a committee was appointed to draft a new Constitution and By-Laws consisting of Hon. Lady Mary Parker, District of Columbia, chairman; Hon. Lady M. D. Hillard, Ohio, Hon. Lady M. L. Freeman, Ky.; Hon. Lady Kittie Terrell, Illinois Jurisdiction; Sir F. J. Richards, Michigan; Sir W. H. Jernagin, Okla.; Hon. Lady Letitia L. Foy, Mass.; and Sir Wm. A. Baltimore, of Dist. of Columbia. The total receipts of this meeting were $60.58.

August 4—6, 1914, the fifth session was held in Pittsburgh, Pa. with twelve Jurisdictions represented. The report of the Constitution and By-Laws Committee was submitted and adopted. The total receipts were $61.61.

August 23—26, 1916, the sixth session was held in Chicago, with eighteen jurisdictions represented "Uniformitory of the work" was the chief topic of discussion and a committee appointed to make research and recommendation upon this subject at the next session. The receipts of this session were $144.33.

The next session was to have been held in Kansas City in 1918 but on account of the World War it was called off.

August 23—26, 1920, the seventh session was held in Cincinnati, Ohio, with twenty jurisdictions represented; but a gloom overshadowed this meeting because of the fact that the Inter-state Matron, Miss Janie L. Cox of the District of Columbia, had passed away just one month prior to the convening of the session. After appropriate memorial service was held in her honor, the principal business of this session was the receiving of the re-

port of the special committee on "Uniformity of
the Work" appointed four years previous, which
report was as follows:
Cincinnati, Ohio, August 24, 1920.

Royal Grand Matron, Royal Grand Patron, and
Representatives here assembled:—Your committee
to whom was referred four years ago, the subject,
"The Unification of the Ritualistic Work of the
several Jurisdictions of our Affiliation," beg to offer the following as a basis of general agreement:

After studying the whole system of degrees and
conferring with others, including the successors
of Robert Macoy, who was the successor of Robt.
Morris, author and founder of the Order of the
Eastern Star, we have agreed that the author and
owner of the works and copyrights, should, ought
to and does know his intentions therein better than
those who would traduce him, and violate their
obligations by injecting innovations into or a sub-
stitute for his works.

1. There is, we believe, nothing in ritualism,
more beautiful, attractive and edifying, when
properly handled, than the Amaranth degree; but
before it was written by Robt. Macoy, finishing it
upon his death bed, as a reward for merit for those
who have become proficient in the other degrees,
there was the Eastern Star, complete in its system
of units, harmonious in its construction, beautiful
in sentiment, definite in its teachings of unadul-
terated Christianity, with the birth, life's work,
death, resurrection and ascension of Christ our
Redeemer as its fundamental principle.

2. Though written or published in 1912, no-
where in it does Alonzo J. Burton, in his history
mention the Amaranth as a working or business
degree.

3. A letter dated August 7, 1920, written by Mr.
J. W. Robertson of the Macoy Publishing Co. reads
as follows:

New York, N. Y., August 7, 1920

Mr. J. C. Scott
    407½ Ninth St., Ft. Worth, Texas

Dear Sir and Bro:—

We regret to inform you that Mr. John Barker departed this life between fifteen and twenty years ago, and we have no means of knowing what his answer to your question would be.

In this section of the country the Eastern Star and Amaranth are usually separate organizations, having separate Grand Bodies, although one must be a member of the O.E.S. before being granted membership in the Amaranth, and we believe that the writers of the Rituals, and founders of the two Orders, intended the Amaranth to bear the same relation to the O.E.S. that the Royal Arch Chapter bears to the Blue Lodge.

However, this is only our opinion in the matter and would not presume to advise you concerning it. It is without doubt a question that only your Grand Chapters can legally settle.

Fraternally yours,
The Macoy Publishing & Masonic Supply Co.,

J. W. Robertson, Per M. D. L."

4. Less than fifty per cent of our members have the Amaranth degree, which under our present system would be either taxed without representation or denied admittance.

We, therefore, recommend that this body work in the Eastern Star degree, transacting its business therein, and use its intelligent influence to induce all Jurisdictions to do the same, encouraging the growth and spread of the Amaranth as an appendant to the Eastern Star.

We also recommend that Macoy Ritual be our recognized standard of work; that Mackey's Jurisprudence be our legal guide and that Grimke's History our official history."

Respectfully submitted,
    J. C. Scott, Chairman
    Wm. A. Baltimore
    Inez T. Alston

MASONIC ORPHANAGE—Americus, Ga.

This report was unanimously adopted; and another committee to revise the constitution and By-laws appointed consisting of J. C. Scott, Chairman; M. D. Hillard, Sue M. Brown; Inez T. Alston and Louisa U. Webb.

August 7—10, 1922, eighth session was held at Washington, D. C., with twenty-one jurisdictions represented; and amount of money reported at this session $457.58, among the recommendations made at this meeting were "That the Grand Secretary of each jurisdiction affiliated with the Conference be requested to send to the Interstate Secretary immediately after the close of its Annual Communication, the names and addresses of the Grand Matron, Grand Patron, Grand Secretary and Chairman of Committee on Foreign Correspondence.

The Interstate Matron, Mrs. Florence E. Scott also suggested a conference with the Grand Masters for the purpose of discussing the regularity of the action of certain Grand Masters in suspending lodges or members of lodges of A.F. & A.M. for affiliating with Chapters or Grand Chapters of O.E.S. which she contended was impeding the progress of the O.E.S. in several jurisdictions.

Mrs. Louise U. Webb, Interstate Lecturer at this session made the following recommendations:

1. The Order of the Eastern Star or Adoptive Rite, stands alone in its beauty and splendor and should be entirely separate from all other orders having degrees as set forth in "Our Landmark" and by Robt. Morris, the founder of the work. If we as members of the Order of the Eastern Star study and practice this work thoroughly and become proficient in demonstrating it, as it should be, there is enough beauty in its ceremonies, without adding or connecting it with any other order, and too, we are working contrary to the wishes of Macoy, who separated the work in his first ritual and caused the Amaranth Degree to be established as an order known as the Independent Amaranth Court. I therefore, recommend that we separate the Amaranth Court entirely from the Adopted Rite.

2. I recommend that all members of the Eastern Star in attendance at our session be properly re-

galed according to the regalia worn by the members of the Order of the Eastern Star. All worthy Matrons, Past and Present should wear the purple sash three inches wide with gold fringe and emblems of the Order if desired and should be worn from the left shoulder to the right side. The Present and Past Worthy Patrons are entitled to wear the same. The other members in attendance should wear the Eastern Star sash, with the five colors, and should be worn from the right shoulder to the left side, the color blue next to the face. The Star officers should wear the color of sash their point represents. This regulation should be practiced in all Subordinate Chapters to cause a better appearance and have the uniformity of Regalia.

I recommend that a committee be appointed at the next Biennial Session to compile a Ritual with the many important items and ceremonies which is not included in the Macoy Ritual.

3. In conclusion I therefore recommend that the Inter-state Conference approve of the important impressive Eastern Star ceremonies as recommended in the "Book of Instructions' for subordinate Chapters, used by the state of Illinois and compiled by Grand Lecturer of the Inter-state Conference of Grand Chapters, and the same be recommended for the use of Subordinate Chapters included in the jurisdictions affiliated in the Inter-state Conference of Grand Chapters of the Order of the Eastern Star.

August 19—22, 1924, the ninth session was held at Pittsburgh, Pa., with thirty-two jurisdictions represented; and the amount of money reported at this session was $558.70.

One of the features of the meeting was a symposium on "Co-operation betwen the A.F. & A.M. and the O.E.S.," the principal speakers being Judge Crittenden; E. Clark, Past Grand Master of Missouri; Atty. S. Joe Brown, Past Grand Master of Iowa; Prof. E. J. Hawkins, Past Grand Master of Kansas and Atty. James E. White of Chicago, attorney for the Imperial Council of N.O.M.S.; Mesdames Lillie Talliaferro, Grand Matron of Okla.; Mary F. Woods, Past Grand Matron of Missouri;

MASONIC TEMPLE— Boley, Okla.

Rosa J. Richardson, Past Grand Matron of Maryland; Etta Hawkins, Grand Matron of Washington and Alice J. Campbell, Grand Matron of New York.

Brother Wm. A. Baltimore of Wasington, D. C., the International Patron, being compelled by illness of his mother to absent himself from the session, for the first time sent the following letter of regret: __

Washington, D. C., August 17, 1924

Mrs. S. Joe Brown
International Grand Matron
Order of the Eastern Star
My dear Sister:

I regret very much to have to state to you that it will not not be possible for me to be present at this conference of Grand Chapters. This will be the first session that I have missed since the organization. But my mother is very sick, and acting upon the advice of her physician, Dr. T. Edward Jones, I shall be compelled to remain near her.

Kindly express my regrets to the Conference and assure the members that I am deeply intrested in the instructive program that has been arranged, and sorry beyond expression that the above circurstances make it impossible for me to be with you on this occasion.

I trust and believe that you will have a very successful session and that all discussions and actions will redound the best interest of all of the Chapters represented in the Conference.

With best wishes for a harmonious, well representative session, and with kindest regards to you and all members, I remain,

Fraternally yours,
Wm. A. Baltimore
International Patron

The "Book of Instructions" recommended at the previous meeting was approved at this session; and the Biennial Address of the International Grand Matron, because of its historic value, was ordered published and the same be used as the official history of the O.E.S. among colored people.

ADDRESS

Delivered by
Mrs. S. Joe Brown
Before Ninth Biennial Conference

Two years ago at our Nation's Capitol, when I received at your hands elevation to this, the highest office within your organization, I felt that I owed you a debt of gratitude, that could be paid only in services to the cause we represent; and the thought most prevalent in my mind was the devising of plans whereby we could make this our 9th Biennial Conference the best in the history of our organization.

Just ten years ago, our International Conference convened in this, the historic City of Pittsburgh with about thirty-nine representatives of about twelve Grand Jurisdictions; and I am sure that the good citizens of Pittsburgh as well as the representatives of the various Jurisdictions who have come here at a sacrifice to both themselves and their Grand Chapters will be eager to note what progress our organization has made during this decade.

First of all permit me to say that anticipating this situation and in order that I might be the better prepared to give out information in response to the frequent inquiries that I was sure I should receive from time to time, in my efforts to inspire those Grand Jurisdictions that had never been represented in our conference as well as to reclaim if possible those that had once been represented but had fallen by the wayside, I attempted to gather all the information possible with reference to the origin and history of the O.E.S. among Colored people in America and elsewhere.

I have found that there was a published record of the Order among white Americans from the year 1857 when Robt. Morris, its founder published his first Ritual down to 1912.

I have also found that there is a published record of Free Masonry among Colored Men of North

America from the institution of the first Lodge under Prince Hall in 1775, down to 1903 but find no mention whatever of the O.E.S. or any other department of female Masonry among our women.

I therefore began a research among those that I thought might be able to furnish me with such information and having failed to find a compiled record or history of the Order, I proceeded to send cut questionnaires seeking such information from the thirty-four Grand Chapters in the United States and Canada reputed to be regular; and also made several attempts to ascertain whether there was a Grand Chapter on the Continent of Africa, and the following communication will disclose our finding:

Monrovia, Liberia, August 25, 1924

Mrs. S. Joe Brown,
Interational Grand Matron, O.E.S.,
Des Moines, Iowa, U.S.A.

Dear Sister:—

Your communication inviting us to the International Conference of Grand Chapters O.E.S. which would convene in Pittsburgh, Pa., August 17th, was duly received. But as it was not possible to send a delegate, the Committee was instructed to send a communication immediately. We regret very much that in consequence of some mis-adventure the letter was not sent, much to the disappointment of our General Grand Matron. However, I am instructed by the G. G. Matron, Mrs. Izetta C. Stevens to write to you, expressing the warm appreciation of herself and the G. G. Chapter to you for the sisterly interest you take in our Chapter.

I am instructed to say to you that the General Grand Chapter will be glad to have recognition in the International Conference and sincerely regrets the lateness of this writing. If you will kindly keep us informed as to the next conference the Grand Chapter will be pleased to be represented there.

We thank you for your kindly interest and hope that we will hereafter always be in touch with the Order of the Eastern Star over there.

Fraternally yours,

for the Grand Chapter,

Sarah R. Freeman

General Grand Secretary.

While en route to Vancouver, B.C., to visit the Tacoma Grand Chapter of the state of Wash., in its 10th Annual Communication; I was awaiting at Seattle the arrival of the Grand Matron Mrs. Etta Hawkins and Grand Patron W. F. Williams of the Jurisdiction and was approached by a lady of the other race, who recognizing my O.E.S. emblem inquired of my identity and my mission; and upon being informed that she was from Ketchikan, Alaska, and lived neighbor to a matron of the O.E.S. whom she was sure would be pleased to have me pay a visit and furnished me with her name and address; and I presuming of course that the matron referred to was a member of my own race, being elated over the fact that I had discovered that we had Chapters and perhaps Grand Chapters in the far away territory of Alaska, opened correspondence with her only to find that she, like my informant, was a member of the other race, affiliated with their Grand Chapter as the following letter will disclose:

Ketchikan, Alaska, November 12, 1923

Mrs. S. Joe Brown,

1058 5th St., Des Moines, Iowa

Dear Sister:—

I am in receipt of a letter written by you to Mrs. Blackmor, a Past Worthy Matron of our Chapter asking for the address of our Worthy Grand Matron.

We, and I think all the Alaska Chapters, are under the jurisdiction of the General Grand Chapter, and our Most Worthy Grand Matron is, as you doubtless know, Mrs. Clara R. Franz, 700 Laura Street, Jacksonville, Fla.

Fraternally yours,

Mrs. C. M. Van Marter, W.M.

EASTERN STAR ORPHAN HOME—
Ft. Worth Texas

On this trip to the Pacific Coast I travelled nearly five thousand miles, passing thru fourteen different states stopping first in Minnesota, where I visited my own, Electa Grand Chapter of Iowa, and Jurisdiction, which includes a portion of Minnesota and which was holding in St. Paul its 16th Annual Communication in Union Hall.

Finding that I was going to arrive in California the 3rd oldest Grand Chapter, too late for their Annual Communication, I wired them a word of greeting and an invitation to join our International Conference, and upon my arrival at Bakersfield, had a pleasant visit at the home of sister Aline Hueston, G.M., who resides in that city and accompanied me to Los Angeles to a platform meeting on Sunday afternoon, where there appeared upon the same program aside from your International Matron, the Grand Matron of Calif., the Grand Matron of Arizona and a Grand Representative of Colorado. Later in the week the Grand Patron of California, who resides in Los Angeles, arranged a joint meeting between the three subordinate Chapters of that city in the beautiful Masonic Temple which is the property of Negro Masons, where we again appeared on a program with the Grand Patron, two Past Grand Matrons, a Past Grand Master of the California Jurisdiction and the Grand Secretary of the New England Grand Chapter, who like myself was visiting the Golden West.

In Arizona where we made our next stop and which is one of our youngest Grand Jurisdictions, a meeting had been arragned in Phoenix, by the Grand Patron, Bro. Clay Credille, who had been advised of our coming by Sister Lynn Ross Carter, Grand Matron and where we were very pleasantly entertained.

We next found ourselves in the Lone Star State, presided over by our Associate International Patron, Bro. J. C. Scott, whose Grand Communication we also missed by one week. However, thru the courtesy of Brother Scott, we were permitted to visit the Widows and Orphans' Home, the pride of the Texas. O. E.S., and also the magnificent Masonic Temple, the pride of the Texas A.F. & A.M., both located at Ft Worth, and in the latter of which we found the office of our official organ the "Eastern Star."

Our next and last stop was in the "show me" state where we found at St. Louis, the Grand Matron of the United Grand Chapter as well as the Grand Matron of Harmony Grand Chapter, also Princess Fannie G. W. McDonald, Captain of the International Conference of Heroines of the Temple Crusades, in whose home we spent a very pleasant evening after a conference with some of the other outstanding characters of this Jurisdiction.

From St. Louis we returned home, but about two weeks later made a trip to Kansas City, Kansas, where we appeared before the Fourteenth Annual Session of the National Association for the Advancement of Colored People and there met and conferred with the Grand Matron of the Kansas Jurisdiction, which is the only Jurisdiction so far as I am advised that publishes its own Ritual.

Enroute to this Ninth Biennial Conference it was our privilege to visit the 35th Annual Session of the Illinois Grand Chapter which was convening in Chicago the week of August the 12th and presided over by Mrs. Carrie Lee Hamilton, this jurisdiction that gave to us our first Grand Matron of this Conference, we found them holding their meeting in Union Masonic Hall of that city the property of the Masonic Fraternity.

Now as a result of this tour of visitation, gathering data whenever and wherever possible, together with the information that I have received by way of responses to the questionnaires, I have been able to gather and now bring to you the following historical data:

About a half century ago, and just one hundred years after the founding of the first Lodge of Negro A.F. & A.M., Bro. Thornton A. Jackson, having received the degrees from a deputy of Robert Macoy, in the year 1875 instituted in the City of Washington, in the District of Columbia, the first subordinate Chapter of O.E.S. as will be found in this volume on page fifteen under the Caption History and Origin of the Adoptie Rite in the District of Columbia.

Just five years later, in the year 1880, in the City of Washington, N. C., Bishop J. W. Hood, organized the first Negro Grand Chapter of O.E.S. followed closely by Tennessee in the year of 1881.

Then came California and others in succession until Grand Chapters of O.E.S. have been organized and now exist among Negroes in thirty-five Jurisdictions including that of Ontario, Canada and Liberia, Africa, each of which is supreme within itself and adopts its own form of ritualistic work, which has naturally resulted in a great variety in the manners of working in the varioius Grand Jurisdictions.

After some years there arose a sentiment in favor of closer union and greater uniformity of work among the several Grand Chapters which sentiment doubtless was in the mind of Mother Letitia L. Foy, whom we all love to honor, when in the year 1907 she called together in the historic old City of Boston, representatives of a number of Grand Jurisdictions and formed this organization that is now known as the International Conference of Grand Chapters of O.E.S.

Today we have in our thirty-five Grand Jurisdictions about three thousand five hundred Chapters with more than a hundred thousand members, having in their combined treasuries about a half million dollars. Aside from many of our subordinate Chapters owning property a number of our Grand Chapters are assisting the A.F. & A.M. in maintaining Masonic Temples valued all the way from seven thousand, to six hundred and fifty thousand dollars.

Many others operate Burial Funds and Endowment Departments which pay upon the death of a member from twenty-five to five hundred dollars. Some have their own printing establishments from which their official journals and other publications are issued; and several have their juvenile Department through which the youth of our fraternity are given burial benefits as well as valuable training in the conduct of business and social affairs.

Now while you are to be commended upon the wonderful progress you have made during these

forty-nine years of your existence, I am sure you
will agree with me that the Order of the Eastern
Star, one of the outstanding factors in the world's
progress, should be a greater force in stimulating
its members to a more intelligent participation in
civic, national and   international affairs,   each
standing out in our several communities for a
practical application of the principles and ideals
exemplified in the characters of our five Heroines.

While as I have already stated a great work is
being done in some of our Jurisdictions among the
youth of our fraternity; yet realizing as I do that
there are many Jurisdictions that have not such a
department and that the boys and girls of today
are to be the men and women of tomorrow and that
upon us rests the grave responsibility of shaping
the lives of these young people, that they shall be
the better prepared to complete the tasks we shall
be compelled to leave undone, I would urge that
wherever it is practicable the various Grand Jurisdictions establish   some form of Juvenile Department such as they have in Texas where they work
under Charter and Ritual issued by the Grand Patron of that Jurisdiction, and that in those jurisdictions where such is not   thought   practicable,
there be organized a Junior Division of the National Association for the Advancement of Colored People in which   Race   History is taught and black
ideals instilled into our young people thus fitting
them for the leadership of the next generation.

And while I would not suggest the taking of our
Order into politics, yet in this new day our women
everywhere should be urged to make use of their
right of suffrage, where they are permitted to do
so and that when they vote not to fail to place in
office men and women who will safeguard the interest of our group as well as the public in general
in both State and National Legislatures, and by so
doing we may do away with the present   status
wherein our National Congress has failed for two
sessions to pass the Dyer Anti-Lynching bill, because as the Senators themselves declare there has
been no demand for such legislation on the part of
their constituents.

UNION HALL—St. Paul, Minn.

During the biennial period, we have received and replied to many communications enquiring for suggestions as to how to adjust all kinds of perplexing problems, some of them arising out of a lack of co-operation between the Grand Matron and the Grand Patron, in most of which cases the Grand Patron has overlooked the fact that the Grand Matron is the presiding officer, and he her legal adviser or assistant, not her superior dictator; and to avoid a recurrence of such we would urge upon the brethren, should there be any such present, that they use more precaution in assuming the prerogatives of the presiding Grand Matron; that they spend a little more time studying the constitutions and laws of the Order that they may get a proper conception of the relative functions of the offices of Grand Matron and Grand Patron and that they not attempt to perform both.

But perhaps the most unfortunate difficulty that has come to our attention is that in several Jurisdictions the Grand Master of A.F. & A.M. seems to have conceived the idea that he is also Grand Master of the O.E.S. and has even gone so far as to carry his contentions in this respect into the civil courts, thus proving to the members of the other race either that our men have no confidence in their women or that we are not yet ready for our own leadership.

Now it is true that our Order was originated by Master Masons for the protection of their wives, widows, mothers, sisters and daughters and hence cannot exist without the co-operation of the members and more especially the officers of the Blue Lodges; and in my humble judgment it is conducive to the strength and growth of both the O.E.S. and the A.F. & A.M., that the most cordial co-operation should exist between these two organizations.

But in some Jurisdictions, notably in Missouri and the states of Washington, Louisiana and West Virginia instead of co-operation we have had the most bitter antagonism.

In each of these Jurisdictions, the Grand Lodge or its officers have gone so far as to organize an opposition Grand Chapter resulting in one side or the other appealing to the civil courts for protection in what they claim to be their rights in the matter.

But the civil courts are always slow to step in and attempt to arbitrate between two contending factions of fraternal or a religious organization, like Pilate when the Jews brought to him their accusations against the Savior which were purely religious, and he attempted to wash his hands clear of the whole matter, neither have the civil courts in either of these Jurisdictions made any ruling that would enable us to determine which of the rival Grand Chapters is the legal one.

In the state of Washington, however, as will be discovered by a careful reading of the "Final Order and Judgment" in the case a copy which was presented to us while on our visit to the Mt. Tacoma Grand Chapter, about the only thing the court did was to enjoin the Grand Master by himself or deputy from further suspending members of the A.F. & A.M. who were affiliated with the opposition Chapter, "except in good faith, after written charges have been preferred against them, and after trial in their respective lodges, in accordance with the procedure in such cases made and provided for in Masonic Laws."

So far as we have been advised there has been no final decision in the Missouri case, but it is not unreasonable to expect that the Missouri court, if it ever decides at all, will in all probability follow the example of the Washington and other courts thus leaving intact the two Grand Chapters in each of these Jurisdictions, each claiming to be the only legitimate one and accusing the other of being irregular or "clandestine," which is indeed an embarrassing situation, and such as ought not to exist; and while we realize that this International Conference is only a "conference," not having or claiming to have any authority to step in and decide which of these rival Grand Chapters is right; yet we do believe that since it is a "conference" of Grand Chapters it is the proper place for representatives of these rival Grand Chapters to come

PANORAMIC VIEW OF INTERNATIONAL GRAND MATRONS

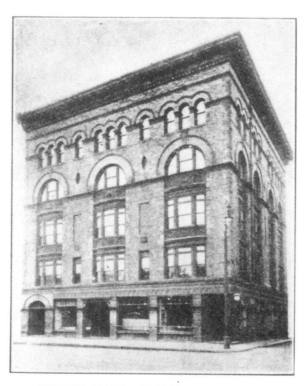

PRINCE HALL   MASONIC TEMPLE
Boston, Mass.

together and confer and that it is our duty as representatives of sister Grand Jurisdictions to lend our influence and good offices to assist them if possible to settle their differences, which it seems the civil courts are unable or unwilling to do.

Hence believing that some good might be accomplished along this line by a free and open discussion here of the respective prerogatives of the Grand Lodges and Grand Chapters, I have given over an hour Friday morning at 10 o'clock to the discussion of the subject "Co-operation between the A.F. & A.M. and the O.E.S. in which discussion I have invited to participate a number of present and past Grand Masters including the two who are accused of overstepping their prerogatives in organizing rival Grand Chapters of O.E.S. in jurisdictions where regular Grand Chapters already existed.

We have also invited to be present and participate in this discussion, each of the male presiding officers of the other International Bodies that are holding sessions here at this time; and while some have already voiced their protest at our allowing the accused Grand Masters to be heard, we feel that they are nevertheless our brethren. We are their wives, mothers, sisters and daughters and believe that no harm and unquestionably much good might result from this symposium.

NECROLOGY

Since our last Biennial Session, the Grim Reaper has invaded our ranks and has robbed us of some of our brightest jewels.

It is therefore with deepest regret that we report the passing of Sis. Kittie Terrill, of St. Paul, Minn., a past Grand Matron of the Illinois Jurisdiction and the first Matron of this International Conference, and Sister Emma Kennedy, another past Grand Matron of Illinois, who was with us at our last Conference at which she was appointed our International Marshal.

On each of these occasions and on the ocassion of the passing of two other members of our Order, who were not members of this Conference, because of their wonderful contributions to the uplift of womanhood and the cause of humanity in general, we sent messages of condolence to the bereaved relatives, in the name of this Conference.

The other two sisters to whom I refer were Mrs. Nora F. Taylor, of Chicago, Grand Daughter Ruler of the National Grand Temple of Daughters of the I.B.P.O.E.W., and Mrs. Mary B. Talbert of Buffalo, N. Y., President of the Frederick Douglass Memorial and Historical Assn., Honoray President of the National Association of Colored Women and the only woman to whom has been awarded the Spingarn Medal of the N.A.A.C.P.

To assist in perpetuating the memory of Sister Kittie Terrill, Sis. Janie L. Cox and our other past International Matrons I have had made and brought with me to this Conference a panoramic portrait containing the likeness of each arranged in order and giving the name of each , the Grand Jurisdiction from which she hailed and the dates that she served you, to be sold at a nominal fee so as to cover the cost of the making of the cuts and the printing.

Having for several years filled the office of Foreign Correspondent of my own, the Iowa Jurisdiction, I find that there seems to be much confusion in the minds of some as to the duties of this office; I also find great differences of opinion relative to the manner of appointing and the duties of Foreign Representatives.

I also find that there is still much confusion in our various Grand Jurisdictions concerning the so-called "higher degrees."

Because of these misunderstandings, much time is consumed and the work of our beautiful Order very much muddled in some of the subordinate Chapters; and since as we have already suggested that one of the prime objects of this Conference is to try to aproach uniformity along all lines of O.E.S. work, we have placed on our program each of these topics for an open discussion, in which we hope to bring out the opinion of the best brains of the Order, which we are sure we have present here and we urge upon those among us of less ex-

PRINCE HALL MASONIC TEMPLE—Chicago, Ill.

MASONIC TEMPLE—Washington, D. C.

perience along these several lines to take the most earnest heed to the opinions of those better informed than ourselves and when we return to our several Grand Jurisdictions, let us put into practice what shall here be agreed upon as the proper method of doing these things; for it is only through some such method as this that we shall ever arrive at anything like uniformity of work.

Those of us who were present or who have read the proceedings of our last Biennial Session will remember that at that session we were favored by the presence and an address of Dr. Wm. Pickens, one of the Field Secretaries of the National Association for the Advancement of Colored People in response to which this conference adopted a stirring resolution endorsing the work of the organization and urging upon the U. S. Senate the passage of the Dyer Anti-Lynching Bill; and pursuant to the spirit of this resolution and in order to' place our organization on record in a more tangible way especially with reference to the Dyer Anti-Lynching Bill in October, 1922, with the co-operation of the good women of our own state, we raised and sent into the Anti-Lynching Fund of the N.A.A.C. P. the sum of two hundred dollars, as a result of which we were asked along with one hundred other men and women of both races who had taken prominent parts in this anti-lynching drive, to give a brief statement for publication by the Anti-Lynching Committee, which we gave under the Caption of "The International Conference of Grand Chapters of O.E.S."

In the early part of the year 1923 we received a communication from Mrs. Addie W. Hunton, another Field Secretary of the N.A.A.C.P., as Chairman of the Committee on Foreign Relations, inviting us to go as a representative of this Conference to the Third Pan-African Conference which was held in London and other points in Europe, suggesting that she was sure you would be pleased to take care of the expense of something like a thousand dollars; and while I knew or rather believed that you were desirous of being a factor in all worth while movements especially for Racial uplift, I felt

that the time was not ripe for us to assume an
obligation quite so great as this; hence I did not
even take the matter up with my cabinet, but did
send a message to the   Conference   bearing the
greetings and best wishes   of this   International
Body.

In Febraury   1924, I received a communication
from Dr. Kelley Miller, inviting me as your presiding   officer to participate in the Sanhedrin or
All-Race conference to be held in Chicago the week
of the 11th of that same month, and appreciating
in a measure the importance of such a movement,
having myself organized on Mar. 10, 1923 and In-
ter-Fraternal   Council   for my   home-city, Des
Moines, Ia., comprising representatives of a majority of the 33 subordinate fraternal   organizations
in that city coming from seven different fraternal
families or institutions, having an object quite similar to that of the Sanhedrin, namely closer contact
between different of our groups, without expense
to this conference and with a view to giving further publicity to our organization, I delegated Sister Louisa U. Webb, our International Secretary,
who resides in Chicago,   to represent us in that
meeting and to report the same to this conference.

My first official act after the   close of our last
Conference was to have printed fourteen hundred
letterheads containing the names and addresses of
all our International Officers and to issue an order
on our International Treasurer in payment of the
same.

I next sent a letter of greeting to each Grand
Matron, apprising them of the achievements of our
8th Biennial Conference and inviting them to be
present at this session, and followed these up with
letters of greeting to the several Grand Chapters
as they met, then   by the questionnaires already
referred to; these with my repeated attempts to get
into touch with Grand Chapters of other continen's
and my responses to the innumberable   communications that have come to this office   during the
biennium have necessitated my sending out several hundred communications in the interest of this
Conference.

RECOMMENDATIONS

I recommend that in the interest of uniformity, the Grand Matrons and Patrons here present pledge themselves that they will recommend to their respective Grand Chapters, that hereafter no degrees be conferred in our O.E.S. Chapters except the five degrees of the Order of Eastern Star, this of course having no reference to regularly organized and duly constituted Palaces of the Queen of the South Courts of the Royal and exalted Degree of Amaranth working under Chapters or Warrants of Grand Bodies of these degrees.

In view of the fact that the Macoy Ritual which is being used by most of the Grand Chapters of our people throughout the United States and Canada, is an exposed work, the sale of which is not confined to members of the Order, I recommend that this International Conference appoint a committee to compile a ritual for our Order to be copyrighted and published under the supervision of this Conference and to be sold only to those known to be members of our Order.

I also recommend that a committee be appointed to publish a history of the Order of the Eastetrn Star among Colored people, to be distributed at a nominal price among our members and any others who may be interested, for by this means, we shall not only be preserving a most important phase of our Race History but shall also attract to our beautiful Order many who are ignorant of its glorious record of achievements of both the present and the past.

In conclusion permit me again to expres to you my profound gratitude for having had the privilege of serving you during the biennial period that is now about to close; in the manifold duties of which I have been greatly assisted by our very efficient International Secretary to whom in particular and to all my International cabinet in general I feel deeply grateful, and while we have not been able to accomplish all that we had hoped we might, we **have done our very best** to live up to the resolution we made upon our elevation to this most exalted station, namely to show our appreciation by rendering service to the cause.

YOUTH OR JUVENILE DEPARTMENT

The followng Jurisdictions have a Youth or Juvenile Department, Texas has 45 Chapters, Georgia 52 Chapters, and California's latest record shows 6 Chapters installed in 1923, while the number of Chapters is not given in latest Oklahoma report the record gives them a membership of 150, and while we have no record of number of Chapters or members in Ark. yet we find that they have also established this Department.

PRINCE HALL MASONIC AND O.E.S. HOME
Rockland Island, Ill.

HOMES AND TEMPLES

Woman has always been known as a home-builder, although the great world knows little of her deeds of heroism, her self-denial and her real devotion to suffering humanity. By experience she knows what it is to be widowed and homeless, therefore she has gladly contributed her part in furnishing and supporting Homes for widows and orphans, and has constantly urged the fraternity to build such where there are none.

Our women as well as our men realize the importance of having a meeting place in which to carry on their activities in which to transact their business and in which to hold heir Annual Communications; hence to this end they have used their clever methods of raising funds, in buying bonds and helpng to devise every possible mean of erecting and paying for Masonic Temples which wherever established have proven not only a blessing to the Masonic family, but a credit to the community in which they were erected.

Of the three thousand and more Chapters dispersed about the globe either alone or with the assistance of the A.F. & A.M. they have made marvelous progress along this line.

Many states like North Carolina, Arkansas, California and others with large Negro populations, have Homes and Masonic Halls owned by the subordinate lodges and chapters throughout the state, and in still others, like Iowa with but a meager Negro population, we find as many as four Masonic buildings although not spacious in their constructon, yet erected or purchased by the A.F. & A.M. with the assistance of the O.E.S. While we have been unable to secure the photo, we are informed that at Jacksonvlle, Fla. stands a Widows and Orphan Home which is the joint property of the Masons and the O.E.S. of that Jurisdiction and is jointly mantained by these two organizations.

At Americus, Ga., we have a Masonic Orphanage, erected in 1898 by the Grand Lodge of A.F. & A.M. with a boy's dormitory furnished at an expense of $14,000 contributed by the Grand Chapter of O.E.S. The inmates of this home which are taught Domestic Science and Agriculture. It has a campus of twenty-eight acres upon which practically all the food stuffs consumed in the Orphanage are raised.

Illinois Jurisdiction maintains a Home at Rock Island, known as Prince Hall Masonic and Eastern Star Home. It is valued at ten thousand dollars. The Masons and Eureka Grand Chapter O.E.S. jointly maintain the Home. It is all paid for and modernly improved. Have owned it ten years.

Eureka Grand Chapter O.E.S. owns property at Harvey, Illinois, worth three thousand dollars, all paid for and is simply a real estate investment which brings a revenue to the Grand Body.

In South Carolina the Masons purchased a building at Columbia which they remodeled into a most magnificent Masonic Temple. It is splendidly situated in one of the business centers of the city, just a few steps from Main Street and within three minutes walk from the Capitol. On the first floor are two large well appointed store rooms, on the second floor seven suits of rooms and a large assembly hall and on the third the lodge room. It is the home of both the Grand Lodge of A.F. & A.M. and the Grand Chapter of O.E.S.

Tennessee, the second oldest jurisdiction maintains at Nashville a Home for widows and orphans valued at $100,000 which home occupies a plot of thirty-seven acres upon which they raise much of the provisions consumed by the inmates of the Home.

The Grand Chapter of Indiana jointly with the Grand Lodge of this state own what they term a Masonic and Eastern Star Home, located in a beautiful grove about six miles east of Marion which they purchased October 22, 1921 for the sum of six thousand eight hundred fifty dollars and upon which they paid the last dollar on Sept. 9, 1922.

Union Hall, a Bldg. put up by the Union Hall Association at St. Paul, Minn. is among the first lodge halls built and owned by Negroes in the Northwest.

It is a brick building containing two full stories above the basement and is valued at $30,000.

The basement contains a gymnasium, bowling alley, show booths and locker rooms; on the first floor there is a large assembly hall with checking room and offices; and, on the second floor lodge rooms in which meetings for both the Blue Lodges and the O.E.S are held.

At Birmingham, Alabama the Masons recently dedicated a Temple which cost $657,704. It contains a basement, an auditorium and galleries with seating capacity for 2000, also six store rooms, four lodge rooms and one hundred fifty-four office rooms.

The Birmingham Age Herald says: "Not only is this edifice a credit to that part of the city in which it is located because of its imposing appearance, but it represents thrift and enterprise on the part of those who made it possible."

There are in this jurisdiction twelve hundred sixteen lodges and chapters with a membership of more than forty thousand.

Dr. A. Baxter Whitby, Grand Master of Masons of Oklahoma Jurisdiction has the following to say by way of appreciation of Oklahoma O.E.S.:

"Strikingly so, do we find recorded here and there in Masonic history the silent yet glowing achievements of our Noble Women of the Order of the Eastern Star and when the records of one Grand Lodge, that of St. John's of Oklahoma, are opened, tribute will be given to women of this our Jurisdiction.

We gladly give credit to the sound judgment and good common sense of the Masons of Oklahoma when they conceived the idea of erecting a Masonic Temple as a Home for the St. John's Grand Lodge of Negro Masons.

The idea was conceived, the plans determined upon and Boley, Oklahoma, a Negro town, the place of location.

With enthusiasm the work began with every prospect for completing the building in the appointed time.

However, it is not always ours to appoint the

time nor season. About 1912 the panic came, the
overtaxed lodges weakened, many Masons became
discouraged and fell by the wayside, murky dark-
ness like a cloud overshadowed us, contractors
threatened and at times seemed as if we would
break in twain. Then it was that the Noble Order
of the Eastern Star of Oklahoma with her 3000
women led by that brilliant enthusiastic and
Christian woman, Mrs. Lillie Talliaferro, our present Grand Worthy Matron, came to the front, laid
down upon the altar all of their many years'
hoarding and said to Grand Master, G. I. Currin,
"We bring you our all and pledge ourselves to help
you to complete the work so worthy begun."

So it has gone from year to year, sometimes one,
sometimes two and sometimes five thousand dollars at the time laid down as an offering from
these worthy women until now we boast of a magnificent Temple worth eighty thousand dollars and
all paid for, 140 by 50 feet, three stories high and
all told a beautiful monument of brick and stone
dedicated to the toil of the men and women of the
Masnic Order of Oklahoma.

Walk into their brilliant Chapter room with me
and you behold the handi-work of these same women. The most elaborate furnishings, altars, desks,
pedestals, the finest of five pointed carpet and
Stars and pedestals to match, and the walls deco-
rated with emblems and columns with arch to
crown all with their glory. Here in their beautiful sanctuary, the entire second floor dedicated
to them alone and cherished so highly by all of
us of St. John's, you find depicted here and there
and yonder their skill in industry, art and song.

The industry is demonstrated in the beautiful
quilts, pillow cases and fancy clothing made and
exhibited from year to year by our young women
in the state.

Their art display of needle work has taken honors at home and abroad and adorns the walls of the
Chapter Room.

The whole is crowned with lovely music and song
rendered from time to time by some of the most
accomplished women of our State who glory in len-

MASONIC TEMPLE—Ft. Worth Texas

ding their bit and take pride in being enrolled as
members. So let's lift our hats again, to our worthy
women who with the other thousands throughout
our Grand Organization in America send up their
their voices in praises   and   cheer as we all go
marching onward and upward and altogether lovely.

At Fort Worth, Texas, the home of our present
International Patron, is erected a modern three
story ' brick Masonic   Temple,   which not   only
houses the Masonic Lodges and   O.E.S. Chapters
but also the headquarters of the official organ of
the International Conference. The Eastern Star,
you will also find in this Temple Fraternal Bank
and Trust Co., a Negro financial institution with
a capital of $100,000.

While in atendance upon   the sessions of   the
eighth Biennial   International   Conference at
Washigton, D.C. in August, 1922 we   participated
in the ceremonies accompanying the laying of the
cornerstone of the magnificent Masonic Temple of
that city which is the result of the joint efforts of
the Masons and the members of the O.E.S.

In October 1924 the Grand Lodge of Illinois with
appropriate ceremonies laid the corner stone of the
new Prince Hall at the corner of 56th and   State
Streets in the financing of which the O.E.S. Chapters, courts of Heroine of Jericho and the Golden
Circle as well as the various Masonic Lodges of
Chicago are assisting; and when our 10th Biennial
International Conference convenes in the city of
Boston in Aug. 1926, the birth place of this organization we shall in all probability be entertained
at the new Prince   Hall   Masonic   Temple, the
property of Prince Hall   Grand   Lodge, the first
Grand Lodge organized in America among colored
men more than one hundred twenty-five years ago
and in the same city where the first lodge was organized among colored Masons with Prince   Hall
as Worshipful   Master, in the   fall of 1775. This
temple is a five story modern brick structure built
at a cost of $150,000, the last dollar of which was
paid in February 1922.

REVISED CONSTITUTION AND BY-LAWS
OF THE
INTERNATIONAL CONFERENCE OF
GRAND CHAPTERS, O.E.S.

PREAMBLE

Whereas it has been clearly demonstrataed that there is necessity for the uniformity of the interpretation of the Ritualistic work of the Order of the Eastern Star in the several Jurisdictions of the Order, and a demand for a closer fraternal relationship among the various Grand Chapters and members of the Order in general, and as there is no supreme body in existance to which the Grand Jurisdictions hold allegiance, we the several Grand Chapters of the Order of the Eastern Star do hereby form ourselves into an organization the purpose of which shall be to strengthen the Fraternal chain and endeavor to bring out a uniformity of the Ritualistic work of the Order, bearing in mind, that the organization dces not assume unto itself in any manner to exercise Jurisdiction over, or assume any powers of the respective Grand Chapters comprising this crganization.

In order to make the foregoing object of the organization effective, we hereby promulgate the following Constitution and By-Laws.

ARTICLE I—NAME

This organization shall be known as and styled, the "International Conference of Grand Chapters of the Order of the Eastern Star."

ARTICLE II—MEMBERSHIP

Sec. 1. The membership of this Conference shall consist of the officers and past officers cf the Conference; all present and Past Grand Worthy Matrons and Grand Worthy Patrons in attendance, of Jurisdictions affiliated in the Conference, together with the past Worthy Matrons of the Subordinate Chapters of the respective Jurisdictions, whose Grand Chapters affiliate in this conference.

MASONIC TEMPLE—Birmingham. Alabama

All past Grand Worthy Matrons and past Grand Worthy Patrons of the International Conference, in good standing in the Order of the Eastern Star, shall be "life members" of the Conference, endowed with all the honors within the gift of the Conference.

Sec. 2. Officers—The elective officers of the Conference shall be as follows:

International Grand Worthy Matron; International Grand Worthy Patron; International Grand Associate Matron; International Grand Associate Patron; International Grand Treasurer; International Grand Secretary; International Grand Conductress; International Grand Associate Conductress.

Sec. 3. The appointive officers of the Conference shall be as follows:

International Grand Adah; International Grand Ruth; International Grand Esther; International Grand Martha; International Grand Electa; International Grand Lecturer; International Grand Warder; International Grand Sentinel; International Grand Chaplain; International Grand Organist; International Grand Marshall in the East; International Grand Marshall in the West; Chairman of the Committee on Foreign Correspondence; Chairman on Jurisprudence; Chairman Committee on Finance.

Sec. 4. The foregoing officers shall be elected, appointed and installed at each Biennial Session of the International Conference of Grand Chapters of the Order of the Eastern Star, and shall hold their office until the next Biennial Session or until their successors are duly elected, appointed and installed, unless he or she shall fail to remain in good standing in their respective Grand Chapters.

ARTICLE III—MEETINGS

Sec. 1. The International Conference of Grand Chapters shall convene in Biennial Session at the same time and in the same city as the Grand Masters Council.

Sec. 2. All meetings shall be opened and closed in the Adoptive Rite or Eastern Star degree; and all business of the Conference shall be transacted in the Eastern Star degree and styled Conference.

This Conference shall not in any manner attempt to diminish or extend any of the powers invested or exercise by Grand Chapters affiliated in the Conference; nor shall any law be created that may effect in a compulsory manner, members of Subordinate or Grand Chapters.

It shall be the effort of the Conference to benefit the Jurisdictions by submitting to them for their own consideration, through their representatives, recommendations, which may be conductive to a uniformity of the ritualistic work of the Order of the Eastern Star throughout our Jurisdictions.

Sec. 3. Votes—Each Jurisdiction affiliated in the Conference shall have three votes on every subject, to be cast by the legally elected representative which shall be the Worthy Grand Matron, Grand Patron or their proxies duly authorized by the Jurisdictions and holding credentials of their Grand Chapters duly signed by the Grand Secretary of said Grand Jurisdiction authenticated by the seal of the Grand Chapter represented.

Sec. 4. The present Grand Officers of the Conference who shall have been duly elected, appointed and installed shall each have one vote on every question.

Sec. 5. The other voters shall consit of the Past Grand Worthy Matrons and Patrons of the several Grand Jurisdictions holding membership in the Conference, who shall have one vote each on all questions except the election of officers of the Conference.

Sec. 6. The voting for election of officers shall be by Jurisdictions and the votes shall be cast as follows: Each Jurisdiction represented shall have three votes two of which shall be cast by the legally elected representatives of their duly authorized proxies; and one vote to be divided among the Past Grand Worthy Matrons and Past Grand Worthy Patrons of the Jurisdictions represented.

Each present grand officer of the Conference and chairman of standing committees shall have one **vote**, provided however, that no member shall be allowed to vote in more than one capacity.

Sec. 7. All present and past Grand Worthy Matrons and Worthy Patrons of the International Conference in attendance of Jurisdictions affiliated in the Conference are eligible to election or appointment to any office within the gift of the International Conference.

ARTICLE IV—REVENUE

Sec. 1. In order to defray the expenses of the Conference and other necessary expenses connected therewith, each Jurisdiction affiliated in the Conference shall contribute biennially the sum of one cent for each member under its Jurisdiction.

BY-LAWS
ARTICLE I—DUTIES OF OFFICERS

Sec. 1. It shall be the duty of the International Grand Matron of the International Conference to open, preside over and close the International Coference at each biennial session. To appoint all committees, unless otherwise provided for, appoint all appointive officers; decide all questions submitted to her; inspect and sign all drafts drawn on the Treasurer. She shall make a report to the Conference of all her official acts at each biennial session.

Sec. 2. It shall be the duty of the International Grand Patron, to assist and advise the International Grand Matron in the discharge of her duties; and in the absence of the Grand Matron and the Associate Grand Matron, he shall discharge all the duties designated for the International Grand Matron.

Sec. 3. The International Associate Grand Matron shall in the event of the death, absence or disability of the Grand Matron, assume and perform all the duties of the International Grand Matron.

Sec. 4. In the event of the death, absence or disability of the International Patron, the International Associate Grand Patron shall perform all the duties of the International Grand Patron.

Sec. 5. The International Grand Treasurer shall keep an accurate account of all receipts and expenditures of all moneys, carefully number and file all vouchers; and make a written statement at each biennial session of the Conference, reporting the receipts, expenditures and balance of money on hand, submitting at the same time the books, receipts, and vouchers for examination by the International Grand Matron and Committee appointed to audit the same.

After the election and qualification of the Treasurer-elect, the retiring Treasurer shall deliver to her successor in office all books, vouchers, receipts and other property in her possession belonging to the Conefrence.

Sec. 6. The other officers shall perform the duties of officers filling relative office s in their Grand Chapters of the O.E.S.

ARTICLE II—STANDING COMMITTEES

Immediately after the installation of the officers of the International Conference, the Grand Worthy Matron of the Conference shall apoint the following standing committees, consisting of five members each, the chairman of each which shall be considered an officer of the International Conference, namely: Committee on Foreign Correspondence, whose duty shall be to perform the usual duties required in the spread of the Order in the various Jurisdictions; Committee on Jurisprudence, whose duty it shall be to examine and report upon all decisions of the presiding officers of the International Conference and all questions of law, that may be referred to them by the presiding officers of the Conference, to examine all propositions, to amend or repeal any provision of the Constitution, By-Laws, Rules and Regulations of the Conference or of the Order, and report its findings with recommendations to the Conference or to the Presiding Officer as the case may require.

Committee on Finance, whose duty it shall be to examine and pass on all bills presented to the Conference and report to the Conference an estimate of the amount to be appropriated to pay the expenses of the Conference; and no appropriaton shall be made until passed upon and recommended by the Finance Committee. To examine the books,

WIDOWS' AND ORPHANS' HOME
Nashville, Tennessee

records and vouchers of the Treasurer and Secretary and report thereon with a stated detail of the financial affairs of the International Conference.

ARTICLE III—SESSION COMMITTEES

Sec. 1. At each session of the International Conference, immediately after the opening of the Conference, the Grand Matron shall appoint the following committees and such other as she may deem necessary to assist during the sessions, consisting of five members each, namely; Committee on Credentials, whose duty it shall be to carefully examine the credentials of all persons claiming the right of membership and vote and report their names and Jurisdictions they hail from to the Conference; to properly list the names of all officers of the Conference and all representatives and proxies of the various Grand Jurisdictions affiliated in the Conference.

Committee to examine all visiting members of the Order present and report on those who are not properly vouched for.

ARTICLE IV—RULES OF ORDER

Sec. 1. There shall be a program arranged for each biennial session of the Conference, under the special direction of the International Grand Matron, of the Conference or a committee appointed by her. The program shall contain the order of business and subjects of papers to be read and discussed during the session.

Sec. 2. All business and reports shall be disposed of before the Conference is closed except such as may by two-thirds vote lie over until the next Biennial Session.

Sec. 3. No member shall speak more than twice upon a subject except by the unanimous consent of the Conference.

Sec. 4. All resolutions, propositons or other matters requiring the action of the Conference shall be presented in writing, signed by the author, to the conference, the first two days, in order that they may be referred to the proper committee, for its consideration, in order that the committee may examine the items placed in their hands, offer recommendations thereon and report on the same before action is taken, by the conference.

 Sec. 5. "Robert's Rules of Order" shall be the paliamentary guide in all cases not ctherwise provided for.

STATISTICAL REPORT

JURISDICTIONS	CHAPTERS	MEMBERS
Arkansas	325	9750
Arizona	6	161
Alabama	429	10000
California	27	1115
Colorado	12	500
District of Columbia	10	2800
Delaware		500
Florida	68	2500
Georgia	435	18000
Iowa	26	1000
Illinois	94	5500
Indiana	48	1746
Kansas	85	2590
Kentucky	86	3054
Liberia		
Louisaina	84	527
Maryland	33	1123
Michigan	23	1200
Mississippi		11630
Missouuri (Harmony)	27	2835
Missouri (United)	21	370
New England	17	790
New Jersey	28	1014
New York	41	2200
Nebraska	9	500
North Carolina	466	11400
Ohio	58	1101
Oklahoma	155	3500
Ontario	6	199
Pennsylvania	48	1900
South Carolina	31	2279
Tennesse	240	5000
Texas	233	6000
Virginia	71	3000
Washington (Mt. Tacoma)	6	347
West Virginia (Sovereign)	35	1690
West Virginia (Prince Hall)		300
	3,434	120,101

GRAND CHAPTERS IN ORDER OF THEIR ORGANIZATINON

The following is a list of Grand Chapters in the order of their Seniority, the numbers prefixed being of existing Chapters:

1. North Carolina, September   1880
2. Tennessee, June   1881
3. California, December   1882
4. Kansas, August   1883
5. Louisaina (No. 1.), June 30   1884
6. Kentucky, August   1885
7. Arkansas, July 12   1886
8. Ohio, August 3   1887
9. Indiana, October 25   1888
10. Michigan, August 21   1889
11. Texas, January 20   1890
12. Illinois, August 11   1890
13. Missouri (No. 1), December   1890
14. District of Columbia, May 24   1892
15. Ontario, April   1894
16. Alabama, June 21   1894
17. New England, November 3   1894
18. Mississippi   1894
19. New York, October 18   1895
20. Maryland, November   1896
21. Georgia, June 3   1898
22. Oklahoma, August 9   1898
23. Liberia, January 24   1903
24. Virginia, July 26   1903
25. Iowa, May 21   1907
     Supreme G. C., August   1907
26. South Carolina, July 10   1908
27. Pennsylvania, November   1909
28. New Jersey, June 24   1913
29. West Virginia, June   1913
30. Washington (No. 1), July   1913
31. West Virginia (No. 2), July 16   1914
32. Arizona, July 11   1921
33. Nebraska, October 15   1921
34. Missouri (No. 2), October 27   1921
35. Colorado, July 24   1922
36. Florida (Date unknown)
37. Delaware (Date unknown)
38. Washington (No. 2.) (Date unknown)

PRINCE HALL MASONIC TEMPLE—
New York City, N. Y.

ANNUAL COMMUNICATIONS

District of Columbia _ __ __ _____January
Liberia _ __ __ ___ ___ ____ ____ _____ January
Florida __ __ _____ _____ _____ _____April
Arizona __ __ _ _____ ____ _____ ____ May
California _____ ____ __ ____ _____ __June
Indiana ____ ___ __ ____ ____ ____ __ ____June
New Jersey ____ ____ ____ _____ ____ _____June
Missouri (No. 1) ___ _____ _____ _____ June
Louisiana _____ ____ ____ _____ _____June
New York _____ ____ ___ _____ __ _____June
Iowa __ _ __ ____ _____ ____ ___ __June
West Virginia (No. 1) ___ _____ ____ __June
West Virginia (No. 2)_ __ _ ____ _____June
Virginia ___ ___ _____ ____ __ _____ July
Pennsylvania _____ __ _____ ____ _____July
Arkansas ____ ___ _____ _____ __ _July
South Carolina _ _____ _____ ____July
Washington (No.1) __ _____ ____ _____ __July
Washington (No. 2)___ ___ _____ _____July
Texas _____ ___ _____ _____ _____ ____July
Mississippi __ _____ _____ ____ ____July
Colorado __ _____ _____ _____August
Tennessee ___ _____ ___ _____ _____August
Ohio ___ _____ __ ____ ___ ____August
Illinois __ _.__ ____ _____ ____ _____August
Oklahoma _ _____ ____ _____ ___ ____ _August
Kansas __ _____ _____ _____ __ August
Kentucky___ _____ _____ _____ ___ ___August
Alabama _ ._____ ___ __ _____ August
Georgia ____ ___ ____ _____ ____ __ ____August
Ontario __ _____._ _____ _____ ____ __August
North Carolina _____ __ _____ ___September
New England _____ _____ _____ September
Michigan _____ _____ _____. ____ __October
Nebraska _____ _____ _____ ___October
Missouri (No. 2) _____October
Maryland _____ ___ __ __ _____ ____November

GRAND CHAPTER DIRECTORY

Arkansas—Grand Matron, Mrs. M. J. Johnson
    Box 94, Arkansas City,
    Grand Patron—H. W. Wheeler
    Box 52, Gum Springs
Arizona—Grand Matron, Mrs. Lynn Ross Carter
    714 Grant St., Phoenix
    Grand Patron—Clay Credille
    1321 E. Madison St., Pheonix
Alabama—Grand Matron, Mrs. Janie Blasco
    152 Lyon St., Mobile   --
    Grand Patron—I. H. Rose
    Box 16, Wetumpka
California—Grand Matron, Mrs. Aline J. Hueston
    1729 Forest St., Bakersfield
    Grand Patron—J. G. Edmonds
    1360 E. 33rd St., Los Angeles
Colorada—Grand Matron, Mrs. Mary G. Clinkscale
    2508 Fremont Place, Denver
    Grand Patron—Samuel N. Nelson
    107 South Union , Pueblo
Dist. of Columbia—Grand Matron, Mrs. Annie M.
    Gray, 628 L St.N. E., Washington
    Grand Patron—Samuel T. Craig
    1646½ N. J. Ave. N. W. Washington
Delaware—Grand Matron, Mrs. Eliza Colbert
    410 Taylor St., Wilmington
Florida—Grand Matron, Mrs. Inez T. Alston
    1611 Lamar Ave., Tampa
    Grand Patron—Dr. J. M. Wise, Tallahasse
Georgia—Grand Matron, Mrs. Viola E. Felton
    Americus
    Grand Patron—Sol. C. Johnson, Savannah
Iowa—Grand Matron, Mrs .Eva L. Abbey   --
    414 E. 25th, Minneapolis, Minnesota
    Grand Patron—Rev. E. R. Edwards, Ottumwa
Illinois—Grand Matron, Mrs. Carrie Lee Hamilton
    Mounds
    Grand Patron—A. B. Dawson, Rock Island
Indiana—Grand Matron, Mrs. Mamie J. Russell
    32 Noble St., Wabash
    Grand Patron—John C. Dawson.
    434 N. West St., Indianapolis

Kansas—Grand Matron, Mrs. Lulu M. Gudgell
720 E. Morena Ave., Colorado Springs, Colo.
Grand Patron—C. B. Walker, Chetopa, Kan.
Kentucky—Grand Matron, Mrs. Sarah E. Peppers
Box 214, Lexington
Grand Patron—Jas. L. Dunlap
108 S. Atkinson Ave., Earlington
Louisiana—Grand Matron, Mrs. A. A. Edwards
1738 Constantinople St., New Orleans
Liberia—Grand Matron, Mrs. Izetta C. Stevens
Monrovia
Maryland—Grand Matron, Mrs. Alice R. Dansbury
506 Somerset St., Baltimore
Grand Patron—Patrick M. Turner
1621 Miller St., Baltimore
Michigan—Grand Matron, Mrs. Mable G. Harrison
115 E. 6th St., Flint
Grand Patron—Wm. R. Evans, Detroit
Missouri (Harmony)—Grand Matron, Mrs. Alma A.
Clark, 2814 St. Louis Ave., St. Louis
Grand Patron—M. W. Wilson
2454 Flora Ave., Kansas City
Missouri (United)—Grand Matron, Mrs. Marie
Hedgemon, 2844 St. Louis Ave., St. Louis
Grand Patron—Robert P. Jackson
395 Farmington Avenue St. Paul, Minn.
Mississippi—
New England—Grand Matron, Mrs. Annie Eichelberger, 64 Sawyer St., Boston, Mass.
Grand Patron—Thomas Coleman, New London
Conn.
New Jersey—Grand Matron, Mrs. Lennie B. Hudson, 614 N. Michigan Ave., Atlantic City
Grand Patron—Pearl Walden
222 Delaware Ave., Jersey City
New York—Grand Matron, Mrs. Alice Campbell
2291—7th Ave., New York City
Grand Patron—James E. Mason, Buffalo
Nebraska—Grand Matron, Mrs. Kate S. Wilson
521 W. 33rd St., Omaha
Grand Patron—Nat'l Hunter
2021 N. 28th St., Omaha
North Carolina—Grand Matron, Mrs. Sallie Evans
619 Orange St., Fayetteville
Grand Patron—Dr. J. E. Shepard, Durham

Ohio—Grand Matron, Miss Ida M. Williams
111 N. 9th St., Columbus
Grand Patron—J. H. Weaver, Cleveland

Ontario—Grand Matron, Mrs. Lizzie Monroe
530 Windsor Ave., Windsor
Grand Patron—W. F. Brown
2329 18th St., Detroit, Michigan

Oklahoma—Grand Matron, Mrs. Lillie Talliaferro
406 6th St., Perry
Grand Patron—W. L. Waid
703 N. 5th St., Muskogee

Pennsylvania—Grand Matron, Mrs. A. E. W. Goldsten, 2126 Heman St., Pittsburgh
Grand Patron—W. L. Winston
1411 N. 3rd St., Harrisburgh

South Carolina—Grand Matron, Mrs. R. H. Walton
Columbia
Grand Patron—E. J. Sawyer, Bennettsville

Tennessee—Grand Matron, Mrs. Ada C. La Prade
910 E. 3rd St., Chattanooga
Grand Patron—C. D. Hayes
Box 243, Arlington

Texas—Grand Matron, Mrs. C. H. Ellis
912 Crockett St., San Antonio
Grand Patron—J. C. Scott
401½ E. 9th St., Ft. Worth

Virginia—Grand Matron, Mrs. Essie C. Williams
723 Caledonia St., Portsmouth
Grand Patron—W. H. Jones
728 W. Marshall St., Richmond

Washington (Mt. Tacoma)—Grand Matron, Mrs. Etta Hawkins, 743 Summit Ave., N. Seattle

Washington (Golden West)—Grand Matron, Mrs. Nina Porter, 1508 E. Garland Ave., Spokane

West Virginia (Sovereign)—Grand Matron, Mrs. Gertrude Brown, 913 Cornwal St., Parkersburg
Grand Patron—Rev. B. S. Dent
P.O. Box 98, Thorpe

West Virginia (Prince Hall)—Grand Matron, Mrs. Mary Harris, Mincar
Grand Patron—Shirley Waid, Wheeling

MASONIC TEMPLE—Columbus, South Carolina

PAST OFFICERS
OF
INTERNATIONAL GRAND CHAPTERS
O.E.S.
1907—1912

Mrs. Kittie Terrell _____ Grand Matron
          Illincis Jurisdiction
Walden Banks   Grand Patron
          New England Jurisdiction
1912—1916
Mrs. Inez T. Alston _____Grand Matron
          Florida Jurisdiction
Dr. W. H. Jernagin_____Grand Patron
          Oklahoma Jurisdiction
1916—1920
Miss Janie L. Cox_____Grand Matron
          District of Columbia
Rev. J. H. Garrison_____Grand Patron
          Iowa Jurisdiction
1920—1922
Mrs. Florence E. Scott_____Grand Matron
          Ohio Jurisdiction
Wm. A. Baltimore_____ Grand Patron
          District of Columbia Jurisdiction
1922—1924
Mrs. S. Joe Brown _____Grand Matron
          Iowa Jurisdiction
Wm. A. Baltimore _____Grand Patron

OFFICERS OF THE
INTERNATIONAL CONFERENCE OF GRAND
CHAPTERS ORDER OF THE EASTERN
STAR
1924—1926

Mrs. S. Joe Brown, Worthy Matron
    1058 Fifth Avenue, Des Moines, Iowa
J. C. Scott, Worthy Patron
    401½ Ninth Street, Ft. Worth, Texas
Mrs. Ada C .La Prade, Associate Matron
    910 East Third St., Chattanooga, Tenn.
W. L. Waid, Associate Patron
    703 North Fifteenth St., Muskogee, Okla.
Mrs. Viola E. Felton, Treasurer
    520 West College, Americus, Ga.
Mrs. Louisa U. Webb, Secretary
    3807 Vincennes Ave., Chicago, Ill.
Mrs. Rosa J. Richardson, Conductress
    1119 Druid Hill Ave., Baltimore, Md.
Mrs. Marie Soanes, Associate Conductress
    2006 North Sixth St., Kansas City, Kansas
Mrs. Lillie Talliaferro, Chairman Finance
    Perry, Oklahoma
Mrs. L. R. Palmer Berry
    4938 Dearborn St., Chicago, Illinois
Mrs. Inez T. Alston, Lecturer
    Tampa, Florida
Mrs. E. E. Burnette, Editor "Eastern Star"
    Cleburne, Texas
Mrs. Marie L. Johnson, Adah. Washington, D.C.
Mrs. Mollie Williams, Ruth, Louisville, Ky.
Mrs. Kathryn Wilson, Esther, Omaha, Neb.
Mrs. Annabel Cooper, Martha, Providence. R. I.
Mrs. Mabel G. Harrison, Electa, Flint, Michigan
Mrs. Alice Campbell, Warder, New York City
Mrs. Sallie Evans, Sentinel, Fayetteville, N. C.
Mrs. Etta Hawkins, Marshal, West, Seattle, Wash.
Mrs. Prudence Penn, Marshal, East, Phila., Pa.
Mrs. Ida R. Harris, Chaplain, Petersburg, Va.
Rev. S. T. Craig, Jurisprudence Committee,
    Washington, D. C.

Mrs. Lynn Ross Carter, Deputy, Pacific Coast,
 714 W. Grant St., Pheonix, Ariz.
Mrs. Elizabeth Monroe, Deputy, Canada,
 530 Windsor Ave., Windsor, Ontario

-- ——

BIENNIAL MEETINGS
INTERNATIONAL CONFERENCE
OF
GRAND CHAPTERS
O.E.S.

Boston, Mass. _____ 1907
Chicago, Ill. _____ 1908
Detroit, Mich. _____ 1910
Washington, D. C. _____1912
Pittsburgh, Pa. _____ 1914
Chicago, Ill. _____ 1916
Cincinnati, Ohio _____ 1920
Washington D.C. _____ 1922
Pitsburgh, Pa. _____ 1924
Boston, Mass. _____ 1926

"Go, History of the Eastern Star,
Where e'er its wandering children are;

Recall to those who hailed its birth
Their toilsome struggle 'mid the dearth
Of cheering words, or sunny ways;
And tell those of later days

How great the triumph it has met—
Lest they forget—lest they forget.
Now in these days of proud progress,
Forgot not those of storm and stress,

Encourage the same zeal and truth
Which marked our Order in its youth,
And let the future years reveal
The same desire for its best weal;

Then shall its record grow and blaze
With the refulgence of its rays,
Till earth, illumined, near and far
Reflects the light of Bethlehem's Star."

THE BYSTANDER PRESS
Des Moines, Iowa.

ABOUT THE EDITORS

Henry Louis Gates, Jr., is the W. E. B. Du Bois Professor of the Humanities, Chair of the Afro-American Studies Department, and Director of the W. E. B. Du Bois Institute for Afro-American Research at Harvard University. One of the leading scholars of African-American literature and culture, he is the author of *Figures in Black: Words, Signs, and the Racial Self* (1987), *The Signifying Monkey: A Theory of Afro-American Literary Criticism* (1988), *Loose Canons: Notes on the Culture Wars* (1992), and the memoir *Colored People* (1994).

Jennifer Burton is in the Ph.D. program in English Language and Literature at Harvard University. She is the volume editor of *The Prize Plays and Other One-Acts* in this series. She is a contributor to *The Oxford Companion to African-American Literature* and to *Great Lives from History: American Women*. With her mother and sister she coauthored two one-act plays, *Rita's Haircut* and *Litany of the Clothes*. Her fiction and personal essays have appeared in *Sun Dog, There and Back*, and *Buffalo*, the Sunday magazine of the *Buffalo News*.

Sheila Smith McKoy is Assistant Professor of English at Vanderbilt University. She contributed to the *Oxford Companion to Women's Writing in the United States* and the *Reference Guide to American Literature*. She is currently at work on a project entitled *White Riot: When Race and Culture Collide in American and South African Apartheid*.